THOUGHTLESS

THOUGHTLESS

GREGORY NICHOLAS MALOUF

Book 2 in the STEP series

Published by Malouf Books, UK

Typeset by www.ShakspeareEditorial.org

STEP series

A place to share and unite in consciousness.
Let's take this next "step" together.

Contents

CHAPTER ONE

SHALLOW LOVE

I have always loved the book *Siddhartha* by Herman Hesse—it inspires me to write. My understanding of the message within *Siddhartha* is best described as follows:

Life is made up of thousands of voices, expressing our own pain or joy, and the pain or joy of those in our life and those outside it—our desires, loneliness, abundance, or greed. Our laughter, crying, singing, sorrow, loss, evil, or good are the river of life—each a part of the perfection of the whole—and we must stop listening to just one voice, but listen to all, interwoven in the river of life. They flow intertwined as life out to sea, and evaporate, turn to rain, and are renewed—this is our lesson! When we can accept the thousand voices as one voice and not listen only to one, we master life!

Thoughtless is a step toward finding inner peace—recognizing that we must accept each other in love and unity; there are many roads but one journey, and we are on this divine journey together.

A Definition of Shallow Love

Shallow love is ego love—a limited view or concept of love contained within an unloved self and expressed in the same manner—albeit without our really knowing. Shallow love is limited or lacking in authentic connection to Self or others.[1] It is important to recognize how this impacts our lives—how many of us have come to express and receive love through the limited expression of our ego-self, born from a modern culture of mistrust or uncertainty.

Often, we find ourselves holding on to feelings of separation or aloneness, no matter who we have in our lives. Shallow love is making a choice to "not know" true abundance … a decision to maintain our fixed beliefs. However, it is choosing to "not know"

---

1 Throughout this book, the term "self" is used in two senses. The inner, all-loving "Self" is indicated with a capital "S," while the "ego-self" is shown with a lower-case "s."

what we already know deep within—that love is the core of our being and our path to happiness—that causes our greatest concern. Shallow love is a conditional love—a love that suits us when it suits us, and in a limited manner, it does! It is how we have learned to express love. This form of expression of love, we have come to believe, is all too real.

When expressed from our fearful ego-self, the love we show to one another cannot truly express the meaning of love—that is, an authentic connection to others. Our discontent comes when we receive the same in return and are left wondering why.

Love is the basis of everything in existence—complete, whole, Self-fulfilling, and joyful; anything less is fear based.

If we look truthfully at our lives, we see that many of our life experiences have not reflected or allowed us to experience "love's" true meaning in a way that could have nurtured our inner Self to express love in return. Our past experiences shaped our thoughts and perceptions, based on a limited understanding of love, and later these perceptions shaped the reality we saw and believed.

It is my hope that this lonely face of the ego-self can highlight how we express a limited view of love to each other—and its subsequent impact on each of us. I hope that you take away with you from this chapter a recognition of what shallow love looks like and what it offers, and in so doing choose to look within and see where love is lacking, and discover the impact this has on you and those around you.

It takes a certain courage to undo past beliefs, assess where we are in our lives, and take the steps required for real and sustainable positive change to occur—a change that we can be absolutely assured will liberate the mind, set us free to experience joy, and project an inner confidence that will be returned in kind.

It is then, in a new realization of where we are in life—what pains or insecurities we carry and what fixed beliefs we are hanging on to—that love, joy, and a remarkable peace follow … that a journey of immense transformation begins.

The Journey to Reconnect Within

If we have in common a belief that we exist in physical form, and are each little more than a body with a brain, each body separate from every other body in the world, existing within a limited time frame, then is it any wonder that we fight, flee, or control every step of our life journey? The consequence of this is our attachments—attaching to people and things to "make" our lives happy. We manipulate situations to get what we want regardless of the impact on others, or we think we need to acquire things—anything to hide the feelings of discontent that reside within. Our constant search for outward stimuli leaves us believing that everyone is out to get what they can. We become transfixed on what we—unknowingly—project. Life becomes a process of bartering: "I'll give you this, but I expect that" goes the daily mantra.

The way we have learned to express love is through our adapted ego-self, using control and manipulation with endless expectations of self and others, to cure a sense of lack, gurgling beneath the surface of our thoughtless and constant actions. These actions create more of the same, yet we become dependent on them. How do we get off the merry-go-round (which isn't always so merry) when the way of life that we have been so dependent on, for so long, is repeated day after day?

The ego-self was created by the belief that we are separate from each other, that we need to control or manipulate others to get what we want. As this perception grows deeper, our communication grows weaker and we feel even more separated from others. We all too easily hide our feelings of insecurity—dare we show any weakness? We push these feelings down deeper and out of sight. We choose not to know, refuse to know; nothing changes and our fears intensify. Here is the role of our ego-self: protecting and defending the image we've made and the behaviors that we exhibit—yet all in vain.

Separation beliefs were shaped by our past teachings (our experiences)—yet even through the fears we have developed in consequence, we seem to still possess a lifeline ... an innate knowing. We seem to gravitate to some level of inner faith when we intermittently recognize or acknowledge the discontent we feel—often, it's when we experience *extreme* discontent that we reach for the lifeline. This is the first step in recognizing our authentic inner Self. In feeling that there must be more to life. For the most part, however, we press on, choosing to remain transfixed by our little world, and holding on to more of the same unease—it feels safer to stay with what we have so long believed in, rather than take a chance for change. *For now, at least.*

When we lose the connection to our inner Self (the lifeline), we effectively act in ways that prevent connection to others—not by choice but rather through the thoughtless expression of our need for love—by not knowing "how" to genuinely express it. It is through this "not knowing how" that our discontent grows.

As the ego was created in fear, its expression must thereby be based on fear. As a result, it can only express an *interpretation* of love.

The way that many of us express love results from the ego-self, and lacks an authentic connection—meaning that love is not felt in the manner we often think we express it. Others are trying equally hard to express their views of life—it's a battle of wills—yet no one is hearing what it is the other person needs. Each is consumed with having their own needs met, and each expects to be heard and responded to.

Love doesn't have conditions, nor does it have expectations—it just communicates … freely, fearlessly, compassionately, with a sense of giving. Love doesn't need to be right, it just needs to be kind. Yet in that simplicity lies our difficulty in understanding. We have become a society where everything needs to be bartered—even love has become conditional. "I'll give to you if you give to me."

It is time to become aware, observe, and reassess our life. It is absolutely vital for each of us, and for the greater good of life, that we seek out answers (or truths), that we start to question our awkward feelings. This is important both for our well-being and for true, authentic, sustainable abundance in this life—our life goal. It is also vital for those we say we love. Asking questions of ourselves is the most integral, fundamental route to freedom, joy, and peace of mind. From inner Self-love and connection, love is expressed genuinely—authentically given and received—and its honesty is felt. Think of a time when you have been in the company of someone who exudes authenticity and kindness. You feel it immediately. This goal is not beyond each of us—it is our birthright and Self-responsibility to reconnect to it. The world we witness daily cannot go on in the same way, nor can each of us continue to live this way. Change is crucial … and fortunately inevitable … it is our life purpose.

Something within you, within each of us, knows love well. It is not a surface whim but rather a deeply felt emotion. That is why we gravitate to it, desire it, and reach for it when things don't go well. Why is it that we have that ability at all? Perhaps it comes from an innate knowledge of how good it feels—a knowledge of the difference between the right way to live and the wrong way.

To deny our search for love can only be our ego making light of what is not—manifesting the illusion that we are all okay, when our reality, if we find the courage to look and ask the right questions, clearly shows us that something is not right.

Every single thought we encounter is governed by one of two emotions: love or fear. And every fear-based thought is governed by the dominant emotion ... love! Every thought, word, and action we speak is governed by the dominant emotion, love.

The only thing that matters, that we each truly desire in our lives, regardless of how it outwardly appears—*is love and acceptance! Acceptance is a consequence of expressing an authentic, loving inner Self.*

We are created whole and perfect, and we are one and the same with everything in existence—we are in effect one soul, all living within a physical realm, to (re)learn the true meaning of love. This could be described as *our soul purpose.* Nature will always find a path to growth, and we are nature's highest consciousness.

How could we not evolve? Everything on earth and within the universe evolves. And if our purpose is to evolve, then what better method could there be than to experience every element, aspect, and possibility of fear through an unloved self, in order to truly know love? Not to know love as some kind of sideshow or some book that must be studied, but rather to "know it as an expression of gratitude and appreciation for it"!

Now, it is easy to disregard this as "throwaway talk." Just words on paper, perhaps? Fair comment when life is rooted in an ego-self; however, it is the ego that will not let love in, in a manner that will transform one's life. This is easily observed by assessing our own lives. Dare we drop our guard long enough to discover love, or ask the questions that the ego dare not ask? "Am I happy or just pretending to be for appearances' sake?" "Am I content and know how to show it?" "What is my life really like?"

Where are you right now in your life—how good do you feel, how good will you feel tomorrow, or the day after? What is for sure ... it is easy to deny how you feel! For most of us, denial is far easier than facing those tough questions.

But we *must* face our reality ... if abundance is truly what we desire. Our lives can be dramatically altered by asking the right questions fearlessly.

It is when we find the courage to face our feelings, observe our behaviors, and recognize that things could be better that a seed is planted. It begins as simply as that ... and in time, the one thing we discover from this process is that the soil is never toxic enough to prevent the plant from flowering.

We either decide to peel back a layer of our false beliefs, by looking for alternatives, or we add another layer by continuing to react to life instead. The difference? Adding a layer doesn't resolve anything and leaves us vulnerable to further (more intense) unease, pain, or hurt when things don't go as we would have them go—and they can't just go as we would have them, because we live on a planet with other people, each with their own needs and wants. By contrast, taking away a layer through observation of our thoughts, feelings, and behaviors lessens the pain and unease the next time a poorly perceived event occurs—that is, when things don't seem to go our way. In other words, we come to understand our needs as well as others' needs. This is what the combination of "awareness" and "truthful new perceptions" does.

If we are vigilant in observing the repetitiveness with which we regress to old ways of thinking and old ways of behaving, then change becomes inevitable. We *recognize* that repeating the same thoughts and behaviors while expecting a different result means that change never comes. The process of willingness—willpower—begins when we physically start to *feel* and then *see* new possibilities.

Recognition of one's reality will ultimately lead to a significant transformation of one's life. It is only when we are not aware that we live blind to truth and continue to suffer.

The wiser we become, the greater the connection we gain to our inner Self; that trust and belief in Self unequivocally removes doubts or insecurities, allowing a loving expression of Self to be projected outwardly instead.

The inner Self knows the answers to all life, because it is divinely connected to this invisible matrix that holds it all together—the divine matrix of life, a fearless, loving glue that makes up all consciousness. It is that inner you that knows at the core of your being the wholeness and loving perfection you were created as and created into. The inner you that is one and the same as every other "you" in existence. In coming to terms with this knowing, through the new feelings you experience, you learn to accept and then appreciate your perfect-imperfections, to accept life and, most importantly, your Self ... and through it, every other. This is the meaning to our lives and the life we have lived—reconnecting and truly knowing love after living a life away from it.

It is when we recognize the meaning to life that we find our life purpose!

A Belief in Separation: Where Our Separation from Self Begins

We can experience trauma from as early as infancy. Its causes can be as simple as the difficulty a parent faces in raising their child. *The expression* on a mother's face, for example, that her baby witnesses ... from one that is all smiles and love, to tiredness and fatigue. There are many ways in which the expression of love can be misinterpreted, and is not for us to blame anyone for them; rather, we must recognize that in physical form there are many ways love can be distorted.

Within my own early family life, the expression of love was completely distorted. But despite the traumatic experiences we encounter in life, and regardless of when they occur, it is vitally important that in our search to find life's purpose and a more free and enjoyable existence, we first find the *know-how* and *will* to authentically forgive our past. No matter how bad that past, until we can forgive—forgive ourselves for carrying the pain, shame, and unease for so long, and forgive those we held responsible—we will not find the peace of mind that literally frees the body and the mind to manifest an amazing life.

Shallow love is our expression of this unloved self—the ego-self. An unloved self is not who we truly are—it is separated from who we are by the lessons we learned early in life, the fears we formed; thereafter we created our ego-self, to help us (in a sense) deal with our perceptions of life. It probably did a good job at protecting us against some of our perceived fears, but sooner or later its fear-based reality and our failure to see the unloved self we project make our lives unmanageable. Poor relationships, misguided communication with others, and the push-pull struggle to get what we can becomes overbearing and self-harming.

The fact is, the greater the distortions of the teachings we have experienced in life, the more significant and liberating our change will be!

Faith starts the process for change—have the courage to ask, "Could there be more?" Ask the question when things don't feel right. Believe there is more, trust and be silent for just a short time. Witness even the smallest change, and any positive impact will manifest a sense (perhaps a mere droplet) of joy and peace, and in experiencing this droplet create in yourself a desire to maintain the faith that anything is possible. Every uneasy feeling or misguided behavior observed is a chance to ask relevant questions, and each time you ask, greater awareness arises.

In physical form, we each meet a crossroad at some point in our life, when life becomes unmanageable. It is a sign-posted crossroad: either turn one way and maintain the ego's damaging effects, or turn the other to find courage.

Our drama in life is our constant search for what lies at the heart of our soul—pure love!

Ultimately, however, each and every one of us will change. Evolve, change, grow wiser ... find our life purpose. The choice of which route to take is for each of us to make at a time and place when we are willing to do so. Yet regardless, almost all of us must reach that crossroad in the end, and turn in the right direction; that is assured. Nothing can prevent nature evolving—and we are nature's greatest consciousness.

We have no choice in this—the power that is everything in existence, of which we are all a part, by its very nature could not operate any other way! If we didn't seek out an alternative to the pain and unease we have come to normalize in our lives, then we would have no hope of the abundance and love we deeply desire.

Our healing and our path to find sustainable love in our life will be "felt" before anything else!

Our minds reason continually in an attempt to justify our many reactions to life and each other—our cries for love are constant, and life just seems to be an endless process of resisting, defending, reacting, needing validation ... It becomes exhausting, and we miss out on so much joy in life. We obscure love and limit the quality of our lives, and the lives of those we say we love, by our expression of an unloved ego-self.

I was taught from a very young age that those who fed me, clothed me, and sent me to school loved me—they were family. So, I clung to seeking love within my family, wanting validation, acceptance, and nurturing when I was feeling hurt, sad, or just bad. Wanting safety and security, a loving connection.

Yet, what I received was a completely distorted version of love—in my early years, love was missing.

Yes, I had a roof over my head, and I had my medical and schooling needs met, and that gave me a sense of security and connection to having a family.

But the experience was not kind. In fact, I couldn't remember many days that were. I was constantly told that I was not good enough; looking back, I realize I didn't receive the love and nurturing a child needs to grow into a healthy adult. All too often, my brother, sister, and I experienced or witnessed pain and trauma through our home life, and as a consequence through events at school or other occurrences. We carry lessons such as those through our childhood and teenage years and suffer insecurities. Our reality mimics some form of that life until we, in our own way, repeat a different version of the same story.

In our house, validation was non-existent and expectation the norm. Rarely, if ever, were my needs and wants met growing up; there was only control and expectation by those who said they loved me, telling me what to do and how important their lives were, suppressing any expression of my own needs and wants. Expression of my true needs and wants would have been taken as neediness or ingratitude, and met with an unwanted reaction. My true feelings, like those of so many, were buried deep within.

When I was old enough to control a bit of my reality, or I thought I was, I swore that I would distance myself from my past. Yet I'd rarely known love (and didn't until my own children were born) nor been mentored in a loving environment, so my expressions of love were founded on a limited view of it. Did I stop to wonder why deep within I carried a constant unease? No, I made sure I didn't, and kept exceptionally busy—becoming more successful was the addiction that drove me ... avoiding the truth was all-important. Doing everything, anything, to acquire a sense of being loved, but doing so without ever expressing my true feelings for fear of being rejected or appearing weak. I believed my past was behind me. How wrong I was, and only time would show me differently. My crossroad would surely come.

EXERCISE
Awareness Check Guide

Here is a simple questionnaire that you can self-score ... If you find you throw the pen away halfway through and swear it is ridiculous then don't continue. But do it honestly, and try to ponder for a minute on any questions that cause you unease. There are no right or wrong answers: awareness is the only goal here.

You should first stop what you're doing, and clear your mind as best you can. Simply breathe deeply into the diaphragm a few times, bring your gentle focus to your breath, and continue to breathe. Once you feel a level of relaxation, ask the questions of yourself, and most importantly be completely honest—you are only admitting the truth to yourself!

Do you feel less than you in your relationships, and carry a sense of insecurity about it?

Do you feel constantly anxious?

Do you feel you need to watch what you say in a relationship?

Do you fear losing a relationship and often demand or expect something from the other person?

Do you feel sad, hurt, or angry or all too easily react to others?

Do you find yourself readily holding resentment?

Do you avoid saying how you feel for fear of being rejected or criticized?

Do you express your feelings calmly or need to delve into dramas and feelings of hurt?

Do you have time to simply chat with your partner or in other close relationships and have things in common to share?

Do you make the effort to find things in common you can share and enjoy?

Do you take responsibility for how you feel or do you find yourself blaming others for how they "make" you feel?

Do you have only limited time for your partner, children, or others who are important in your life because of all the things you do outside your relationships?

Are you afraid of losing a relationship, and unwilling to adequately and calmly express this in order to make changes, choosing instead to maintain the ways things are, no matter how bad it feels?

Do you think about what the other person might need or are you fixated entirely on your own needs?

Do you make time to discuss your needs and other people's, and thereby put reason and understanding to each person's actions or reactions?

Exercise continues on next page

Exercise continued

The ability to hear the answers to authentically asked questions, when we take a few valuable moments to observe how we feel, comes from our instinctive Self.

It was hard for me to do this at first—my ego-self wouldn't allow me to recognize my true feelings or observe any behaviors of mine that showed there was a problem. I spent life denying I had a problem or blaming others for how I felt.

Scoring

This is an exercise in feeling your true feelings and observing your behaviors. It is important to note that there is no wrong or right score. The perfect score is one that helps you become aware of what it is you are feeling and able to observe the behaviors that have kept you in a state of unease, often unbeknown to you. Past teachings conceal what you think and feel for a myriad of reasons. The reasons are less important at this stage than the recognition of your true feelings.

Scoring yourself is a process of first "feeling" where you are within a relationship, and in the absence of feeling "observing" your behaviors—they will point toward your feelings. Unease can be expressed in many ways—readiness to react, anger or outbursts, aggressive actions, continual judgments and criticisms, behavioral volatility, anxiousness, restlessness, insomnia ... Question any unease you feel, but it's important to do so wherever possible without blaming others.

Look within—ask, observe, and simply become aware! For now, it's a good start!

In this state of feeling your unease or observing your behaviors, there are three things you can choose to do:

First, you can simply accept where you are in life and maintain the status quo. If you decide to maintain your current reality, then try to do it completely without blame or regret. If you blame, criticize, or judge, you will only end up in the same place looking for the same answers further down the trail, and your old patterns of behavior will limit the love you feel and express in life.

Second, you can decide to talk about this with your partner or another person you're close to. It's often difficult to begin authentically expressing yourself … Discussing how you feel is an expression of your authentic Self—in expressing your inner needs and want, hurts, and pains, be prepared to be met with all your old fears. Our path to peace of mind is often blocked by those we have attracted into our life whose personalities match our past comfort levels. To break through this barrier, as the world you perceive begins to change, takes courage. And change is the ego's greatest fear. "Hold the line!" calls the ego; the pain is what you know, and it comforts you, when all it really means is "I'm in control … I'm safest this way, however bad I feel."

But change must start somewhere, and it starts with owning your reality, identifying it, and fearlessly expressing your true needs and wants.

Third, you can move away from the situation and allow the other person in the relationship time to ponder their own reality. Remember, this is about you, and the process starts with you owning your truth. In a relationship where the other person cannot listen or accept your reality, you need to set a boundary with them. If they cannot hear that you need to express your authentic Self or that you will no longer accept being manipulated or controlled, then it is important to put distance between yourself and their energy.

Leaving people who won't listen to you, or accept change as you have, to ponder their own thoughts is, as you will come to see, vitally important for you and for them … it is in itself an expression of love. There are, however, many options we can explore before taking this measure, so it is not to be done in haste.

Awareness gives us choice—choices we didn't think we had!

I started with a lie that I needed to be perfect and lived a lie where I appeared to be perfect!

In my own case my attempt to express my authentic Self was met with resistance from my family of origin; they chose to stop communicating with me in the hope I would conform and be silenced. Truths have an uncanny way of making people feel uncomfortable. If people are not comfortable within themselves then why not give them a mirror? Truth is a mirror. My well-being, and thereafter that of my children, and my passion to help others were too important to be silenced by the fears of others. I opted for the two Cs—courage and change.

Trust in Nature's Gift

Shallow love is nothing more than a *cry for love*, because we just can't seem to find the "sustainable" peace and joy—love's gifts—that we desire above all else.

Peace and joy are attributes of love—and love is the divine matrix of all life—and that is why we seek out these qualities in life relentlessly. Who doesn't want peace and joy? With peace and joy, what do you have? One could argue quite easily that you have everything!

Do you love it when you are being pampered in some way, even at a day spa? Do you love it when you finish an authentic conversation with someone who was previously a stranger—feel something empowering in the connection? Do you love that moment when you are alone at the end of a hard and productive day at work where everything just seems to fall into place—the peace you feel? Do you love it when you give time to *you*—a moment in silence? When you have a chance to do something totally off the cuff, new and exciting? Visit a new place? When your day is changed by a smile, or someone does something unexpected that helps you in a small way? When you enter a relationship that is open and vulnerable?

All too often, we dismiss these acts of loving kindness, these small blessings to oneself and others. We don't seem to hold on to them or remain grateful for them for more than a moment in time—yet we wish there were more of them, feeling a constant need for something that actually we have in abundance. Wishing and wanting—the roller coaster—yet not holding dear ... receiving and dismissing; for our fears, more is never enough.

Yet each of these blessings needs just a little more of our recognition and gratitude, to create momentum away from the limitations we put on our lives. When we deny these moments of joy, then once again our past is interfering in our present!

If we do not value these small blessings in life, what hope do we have of sustaining them? Gratitude is the greatest catalyst of growth and abundance. Gratitude enables many of life's simple pleasures and magnifies them. Our projections of anything less curtail them.

We are only ever motivated by love or fear. How do you wish to be motivated?

If we change the thoughts behind our perceptions, learn to be "aware" of what brings us peace and joy and what does not, we begin to notice our behaviors and how those behaviors make us feel. In this understanding, developed with practice, our inner Self-knowing aligns with those expressions of life that mean something, instead of the reactionary needy behaviors that do not.

Until we face our fears and recognize where they originate from, we can never find sustainable love in our life, nor the joy and peace that follow it!

We all must recognize that there are many injustices in the world—situations where people are not given the opportunities that so many others have; however, assuming we believe in something greater than the physical existence we witness, are they not engaged in bringing about their own justice, and realizing a life purpose of their own? If our view remains limited, very little of what we witness in this world makes sense, and this is why so many despair. We have all witnessed the plight of those whose options appear utterly limited and unjust—yet their courage can unite us and lead us to question what is being expressed in their life experiences.

Many of us, however—those of us with so many of life's pleasures at hand, and with many opportunities available to us—need only to recognize that the world we see is simply created by our thoughts before we can turn things around—instantly, in some cases. This is achieved by deciding to face our reality honestly and take responsibility for it—by considering that maybe we can truly change, maybe we are responsible for what occurs in our lives. The purpose of life is to evolve.

Look back and realize that, somewhere in your past, each negative thought was created by an experience. Facing these experiences is like peeling back the layers of an onion—we are able to remove them, one by one, through awareness, and in this way move past them.

Separation belief is our past holding on for dear life ... the past that created the fears that distort our thinking and manifest fear rather than love—a love we feel undeserving of. Separation belief ends with self-forgiveness, and self-forgiveness starts when we are willing to plant the seed through awareness and observation—when we courageously learn to face the truth of our reality and are willing to substitute love for the fear we thoughtlessly express instead.

Removing Separation Belief from Your Life

1. Understand life's meaning—that we are all here to experience every aspect of fear in order to truly know love. We all have a divine purpose and are all inextricably linked!

2. Be aware that each of us has the same intrinsic desire—to acquire and sustain love and acceptance in our life—our most joyful moments are when we connect.

3. Be aware that your peace of mind is directly linked to that of your partner, children, neighbors, colleagues, and friends—in short, to that of each and every other. A quick test—next time you judge someone, criticize, or blame, ask yourself afterwards, "Do I feel better or worse?" On the other hand, the next time you offer love or kindness to someone you never thought you could, ask yourself, "Do I feel better or worse?" You will discover the answer for yourself.

4. Learn to master observing without evaluating! Let others hold their reality, and always hold yours. Don't react— allow all that happens to happen! Repeat daily when you wake, "Today I will not react but merely observe everything around me."

5. Have faith that your thoughts determine your feelings— and that you can change those thoughts in an instant—by the choice you make! No matter what the situation is, you can feel better. Your feelings will lead to more positive actions that return in kind.

6. Connect within to the silence of Self, and learn to send loving thoughts to any perceived threat ... do it regularly and see what occurs. Be mindful of what occurs.

7. Share what you wish to receive. Do you want love? Offer love. Peace? Offer peace. A smile? Offer a smile.

8. Recognize that our past teachings are lessons in ways to recognize, forgive, and grow wiser—be excited to learn from them what is possible and what gifts await.

9. Choose one of the three options above (accept, express yourself authentically, move away) when faced with challenges within your relationships.

It is only when we look within that we can remove the limiting beliefs we have learned so well!

How do we improve our relationships immediately? Let me share some thoughts:

1. Observe without evaluating—make no judgment about what the other person is saying. Simply (or not so simply!) do not react, just observe. In time you will come to learn that other people's reactions are nothing more than their call for love.

2. Know that the other person is expressing their reality—if you react you will then be expressing yours in reply—it's a bit like a tennis rally, with reactive volleys occurring until someone gets the upper hand. In the end, however, unlike in a tennis match, there are no winners. Let others express their reality—do what I have come to term "hearing with your eyes."

3. When you are about to react, remember to ask yourself, "What would love do now?" If this isn't working for you and you are still ready to react, then reason with yourself that there are no winners when we react in the heat of the moment, and choose instead to be "kind instead of right."

4. Know that the other person has a past just like you, and any reaction they make is an expression of the fearful experiences of that past. Their ego-self is (re)acting out a hidden fear.

5. Remember that all of us have two primary desires: to be loved and accepted—allow others this love and acceptance, regardless of how hard it may be at the time. In that instant, feel how good it feels to allow others this through something you say or do, and regardless of their reaction being good, bad, or indifferent—the gift of giving is your part done!

6. Discuss your true needs and wants openly and honestly and be prepared to listen to your partner or others. If their reaction is one of shock, criticism, anger, or blame— simply stop! Try another time when things are less heated and reason is allowed to prevail. Most of us have buried our needs and wants within us for too long—we can choose to make this first step authentically.

7. Know you have the power to discuss any unresolved issue—do so without appearing to blame the other person! Similarly, do not blame others when they vent or express their reality. This is vitally important! To reiterate, keep your reality for you and allow their reality to be theirs. If it gets personal, reactions will be triggered and the discussion will remain unresolved.

8. Know that, even in very challenging situations, you always have the power to make *some* change. If you cannot make sense of the nonsense and the other person simply can't hear what you are saying, either do what you can to move away from the situation (physically or psychologically), or remain and accept it. Make a decision and stick with it.

9. Remember to be fearless in expressing your hurts and how you feel, and, importantly, ask how the other person feels. If we learn to overcome our initial resistance to our feelings and express them openly without blame, we will in time allow others to face their feelings too. Yes, it is awkward at first!

10. Remember the good qualities about the other person in the relationship. If you have any negative thoughts—for now, just drop them! Your reality is your reality: take responsibility for it, own it, and leave the other person's reality with them.

What do you want out of life … peace and joy? Then act in ways that will deliver them … through new actions—the thoughts to sustain them will follow.

Our willingness to share kindness and love unites us … This sharing often defies our past teachings—the teachings that caused our separation beliefs. What will you now share—more fear, or more love? The choice is solely yours to make. What you give is what you will receive.

Embrace the small things in life that bring you joy, peace. Gratitude for them will bring more of the same to you. They will act as stepping stones against the turbulent current we often feel we are experiencing until we reach this place of understanding.

Life has incredible meaning, and our relationships are our greatest catalyst for change. It is within every relationship that the seeds for growth are planted.

Extending love is our life's purpose and the natural evolution of our soul.

CHAPTER TWO

TUNNEL VISION

"A feeling that greater possessions, no matter of what kind they may be, will of themselves bring contentment or happiness, is a misunderstanding. No person, place or thing can give you happiness. They may give you cause for happiness and a feeling of contentment, but the joy of living comes from within."
Geneviève Behrend (1881–1960)

When you play a video game, you focus your attention on beating the game—but the game you play is programmed to beat you! You play the game again and again, playing and losing, in an attempt to win at last.

The game is programmed the same way our egoic state is programmed—you project your ego-self into a game, and you win and lose. This is the game of life. It is the purpose of life to recognize the game, and this gives life its truest meaning.

The ego is the computer chip, the twenty-first-century chip that is doing a very good job of messing everything up—at least that is how it can be perceived.

The ego has brought us to the point where we witness a world of people in crisis, not recognizing the life purpose that is so vital in discovering the path to abundance. The game is beating us and we must each take responsibility for turning the corner.

If we do not change course, the consequences will be much more severe within the coming decades as our collective thoughtlessness elevates pain and fear exponentially. Modern technology can amplify our fears, as many of our behaviors over the past forty years have demonstrated. Yet encouragingly, through the same technological media we have the power to significantly spread the seeds of transformation.

Our individual paths affect what happens to us all globally because each individual has the power and influence to impact others. Change starts with our singular actions; it starts by each of us taking responsibility for their thoughts and behaviors and recognizing that those thoughts and behaviors are not bringing about the desired results.

The pain, fear, and anxiety of so many is evident—fewer and fewer are content with the way they live. Nearly all of us are fed up with how we see the world, and how it psychologically or physically impacts our lives and the lives of those we love. Burdened by past experiences, we can easily carry on through life, perhaps feeling moments of happiness, yet rarely content no matter what or who we have in our life.

We long ago lost faith that our lives are being well guided and we are often left feeling unsafe, lacking confidence in life, feeling alone in our responsibilities, or abandoned—and, worse, perceiving very limited meaning or purpose in life. This creates lack. In this lack, our unmet needs and wants come to the fore, obscuring our vision further, leaving us unable to find solutions and amend our lives in a way that would be sustainably fulfilling and abundant.

Yet amid the turmoil we can still somehow feel that there is hope outside this mad game playing out all around us. What is it? ... Do we dare ask? Perhaps our inner, instinctive Self is talking to us ... still, however, our thoughts are too loud for us to hear the answer ... for now at least.

We carry with us our past lessons and put into positions of power (in government and business) people who follow the doctrine of the same fears we grew up with. It is now, however, that many of us are gathering momentum, starting to ask relevant questions, and expressing our discontent with the state of play because the world we experience neither looks right nor feels right.

We look for change. We desire change. Yet many are too afraid to do anything about this perceived reality. We hope against hope that it will just correct itself. We are caught up in our own tunnel vision, in a mindset focused on beating the game—or, as it could best be described, winning against the odds we *perceive*.

Things just don't feel right—they haven't felt right for a long time—yet what do we do about it?

TUNNEL VISION is formed by the obsessive thoughts and behaviors that manifest (selfish) emotional neediness, ultimately driven by past fears. I call this one of the many faces of the ego. It involves going over the same thought processes repeatedly, hoping for a different outcome. As a consequence, we may "do" relentlessly—think, act out, and carry anxiety as a companion to avoid any realization that something may be wrong. We readily deny any negative feelings we experience in an effort to dispel our poor perceptions and prove we can win this game.

Tunnel vision is an excuse for not facing our truths—the truths behind the reasoning behind the unease and discomfort we live with. Tunnel vision keeps us in an unconscious state, attaching determinedly to people or things, as if we were wearing blinders, in the hope they make our life better.

We choose to think obsessively, react instantly, or do relentlessly from emotional neediness, and we have come to normalize this as part and parcel of life. We live in our past and react to it (miscreate), rather than passionately taking action in the present (creating).

Tunnel vision is our defense against any perceived threat to the illusionary self and the illusionary reality we have created. To this illusionary mindset, anything and everything can be perceived as a threat. We fight or focus in all manner of ways to keep the threat from engulfing us.

Tunnel vision derives its power from those past experiences that have created a sense of lack in us. A sense of lack miscreates a *selfish* emotional neediness, resulting in us forming attachments to people and things in our quest to win the game—and as a consequence blocking ourselves from forming authentic connections with others. It becomes our quest to seek from those attachments more than we could gain. This then suppresses present-moment passion for life in favor of needy obsession, devaluing our lives in the process.

In my own life, I would work up to sixteen hours a day—all to escape my past. My constant anxiety and 3 am wake-up calls ensured I found an escape of some sort. Based on my past, I reasoned that if I acquired enough money I would never again be in the situation I had been in while growing up. Tunnel vision was pushing me toward a perceived success in life (creating my needy attachments)—with little thought for a structured and balanced life that included those closest to me. In truth, in hindsight, I came to realize it was a form of escapism—a denial that my past existed at all and a belief that fighting for survival was the only way to live.

Even when I slept, I dreamt often and awoke restless. My thinking would repeat itself over and over. My mind was living in the prison of my body, stuck in anxiety and the fear of not doing or not having enough, the need to fixate on someone or something—to "keep the wheels turning" and be successful!

Passion, on the other hand, derives its power from contentment … and contentment comes from living in the present, from the love of doing enthusiastically without an emotional attachment to the outcome. From learning to value what we have now. Learning by facing the truth, by asking the right questions to start a different thought process. Changing perception from a negative state to a positive one, simply by looking squarely and honestly at the moment, then being "willing" to change, the effects of which will be felt almost instantly. However, I was too afraid of change—this was too great an ask at the time. To be asked by limited ego-thought to value what I had in life then and be grateful for it, in order to thereby manifest more of it? That was too hard a pill to swallow—I had no trust outside of my limited view, my own distorted opinions and beliefs.

When I reached a crossroad at age fifty, after suffering considerable trauma in my life, and began to write, I also began to reassess honestly where I was in my life. I became so enthusiastic about expressing on paper my life lessons … It was cathartic in every sense … it became a purpose, then a passion to discard old thinking and thereby find a way to live in the present with greater acceptance of life, rather than simply reacting and needing to control every outcome.

Life started to show me meaning. I was consciously aware, and my senses were alert. By facing my truth—the truth of why things went so poorly for me and my family at a point when I genuinely thought I was beating that game—was something I felt I needed to share. In a way, it was a need (expressed as passion for doing) to live authentically and give more of myself to others. This was something I thought I'd always done—but in reality had not. I learned to begin to release the past and the hidden subliminal messages that caused constant uneasiness within me, and I found an invigorated passion for just letting go and accepting more— it was liberating to feel something other ... whatever that other was ... supporting me! I wanted to share these new feelings and thoughts, and, importantly, the freedom and joy that followed.

... Like the joy of starting a new job, or the excitement of a new relationship ... and with my new sense of purpose ... I was also motivated to write to help others—especially the ones I loved—to not go through what I had because of poor perceptions born from early life lessons. To share with others in the hope they would find their own knowledge of "how to do it," to equip them with the tools to trust in Self (their greatest mentor) ... and journey well through life no matter what conditions they faced.

Our subliminal justification for tunnel vision is that we have no time, and we carry too many fears to face the truth of our lives— with our past firmly in control and limiting our ability to live freely and joyously in the present.

It is only when we live in the present that we find the innate strength to truly live life. When we live life, our passion and purpose intensify.

Our individual discomfort and unease affect us all in one way or another, often leaving us mentally exhausted and lacking in passion, and downgrading the fundamental life ingredients of joy and bliss, which we so richly deserve, to fleeting moments of happiness.

I would find myself working till late and rising early. My wife and I had little time together. The time we had had in the early years disappeared due to responsibilities at home and at work—I would work around the clock, and my wife would clean and look after the kids around the clock. From the outside looking in, I'm sure it seemed we had the perfect life—and although we did in many respects, neither of us looked at what we had but rather at what we felt we had to do instead! This period, void of authentic connection, would take its toll on our family. In time, our lack of gratitude and appreciation would manifest exactly what we sowed—my wife and I grew apart ... the family broke up.

The ego has little or no belief in Self-love—while it may appear to have it in abundance, it does not. The ego's need to exalt itself or to attach to external things or the company of like-minded individuals to justify its "winning" reality leave no room for inner Self-connection.

If we wish to have peace in our life and to enjoy life as we desire it to be, we must learn the lesson of valuing what we create and enjoying the journey along the way, rather than "attaching" to the image we create and to *what we think we need* to prop that image up. "Detaching" doesn't mean going without—it means taking away the emotional and psychological neediness that drives our tunnel vision and devalues our life. Emotional neediness leaves no room or time to enjoy what we have.

Attachments to—emotional neediness around—people or things will take away the enjoyment of them. Created by our sense of lack, attachment leaves us forever chasing perceptions (ideas—nothing else) of *what we think we need* rather than appreciating what we already have, in order to heighten our sense of self.

Learning to detach was one of my biggest challenges—I simply couldn't let go.

In hindsight, I must have felt abandoned or worse from a very early age. Both parents worked, and ours was a highly volatile family environment. As far back as I can remember, my siblings and I lived in the shadow of abuse. Father, with an addiction to gambling, would determine the volatility we'd all experience each day. Later he would use humor to compensate for his wild reactions. Any relief was welcome. There were outward pleasantries in the public arena, and inner pain and trauma expressed in private.

My life was playing out with nothing other than tunnel vision. My inner urge to distance myself from my painful past was all-important. The more successful I became, the more focused my tunnel vision became—and the more I felt I was succeeding in distancing myself from the past.

In truth, the past remained hidden and unresolved, and I was acting out that past in so many ways—addictive behaviors, having little time for loved ones, believing what I did was for them, lacking gratitude for them or for what I had acquired—constantly looking for more. In essence, repeating my past as I learned, albeit in a different way, to play the game ... gambling my life on business, on workaholism, which kept me from valuing almost all of it ... reinforcing the lie in which I lived.

It was only when I started to connect to Self, identify the truth behind why I felt so ordinary much of the time, that I knew change was needed. It was when I forgave myself, forgave myself for carrying my distorted lessons for so long, that I found the courage to ask, "Could there be another way?"

It's important to note that repeated regression to old behaviors, with the added ingredient of "awareness" (which will occur often once we realize that perhaps there could be another way), is a vital and integral part of freeing ourselves from our burdens—in other words, getting the mindset right. It is through awareness we begin to realize we are responsible for our lives, and the thoughts and actions we take thereafter will begin to change.

It was through awareness that I stopped my self-criticism and self-loathing following my marriage breakdown and family break-up ... the fear of failure that had driven my tunnel vision was now being reassessed. I realized this was my challenge and mine alone. I knew I needed to take things more slowly, nurture that wounded child within. I started to appreciate what I had achieved in my life—in other words, I started to value who and what was in my life ... and not outside it—I stopped constantly looking for more of what I already had in abundance. The relationship I held dear was gone in those moments—however, it should be said that that relationship later returned on a different basis, as a much deeper friendship ... I just needed to heal myself, in order to accept and release the past.

From this inner Self-awareness, we come to recognize that the more we give away, the more we receive in kind. When we begin this new journey, it is important to be aware of what we give. Do you want more love? Offer it to others. Do you want your children to be honest with themselves? Be open and honest with them— tell them how you feel. Do you want your relationships at work to improve? Then start the process yourself—don't blame or judge, send different signals. It is time to let go of our past beliefs and the fear that has held us to ransom.

As I experienced more "awareness" that I was "willingly" desiring, whenever past fears would raise their ugly head I would simply observe my feelings to see my reality and keep any behaviors in check. By recognizing feelings of uneasiness, I could change the thoughts that incited poor behaviors and came to realize the incredible benefits that awaited me when I did so. For example, the miracle of mending relationships I'd never thought I could, and breaking away from relationships that were toxic yet had previously filled the void. It was *seeing* the miraculous results from the new actions I took that kept me doing more of the same. It was choosing peace of mind that allowed me to really start to live life, take risks, venture forward in ways I never had, and accept challenges as a chance to emotionally evolve and access a real sense of joy. I did not forget the past but I certainly began to *forgive* the past, and I began to encompass immense feelings of freedom within.

I have been blessed to have lived both extremes in my life.

Through tunnel vision and dogged determination I created enormous success and wealth—all driven by self-made fears. Yet I neither enjoyed life nor the people and things within my life to the fullest extent.

Consequently, I discovered the power of detachment—if I wanted to heal, I had no choice. Without attachment, I learned some very important lessons—I learned that the people in my life, especially those closest to me, and the many things I had acquired should be appreciated and valued during the journey. In other words, I needed a life driven by gratitude, rather than the lack of gratitude I had shown, albeit unknowingly.

By realizing the misgivings I had in attaching, I learned the art of detaching. In this knowledge I genuinely felt gratitude for my past life ... I recognized that the lessons I had experienced early in life were no longer there to be condemned or feared, but rather ACCEPTED AND RELEASED. My reward? The wisdom that came from those experiences—the freedom and the peace of mind I could then feel consistently.

Our impatience, our need to control every aspect of our lives by demanding what we think we need, is nothing more than poorly perceived "wanting," which leaves us forever unfulfilled. In our non-acceptance of our higher Self, we rely on all things outside Self and manifest more fear through the ego as a consequence. Yet the end result never seems to be a sustainable and desirable outcome.

Instead, if we live fearlessly within the present moment we instinctively know that what we need is all those things that create in us more love, joy, and peace—it is the secret to abundance. Nothing is going to attract to us that which we deeply desire if our wishes are disguised by our past needs and by the ego-self in all its unwillingness to truly detach and surrender past beliefs.

So, it is important to remember that the power to consciously create is the power to do the following:

- Detach from things you obsess over by making a decision to do so.

- Become conscious or aware of any neediness or selfish emotional attachment by recognizing your behaviors and deciding to let go (even if that action doesn't last long—it is the attempt that matters).

- Remain in the present so that your natural creative and imaginative Self can know what it is you truly need. You do this by being *vigilant* about your thoughts and the actions that follow. When you feel unease, you are not aligned to your true Self, but rather a past experience. Let unease (fear-based thought) become your early warning signal that a new thought is needed. Learn to become ultra-aware of this signal.

- Realize that new thoughts come from new actions. Do something that is bigger than a negative thought process you are experiencing—write in a journal, begin to write a book, give someone support, do something positive for someone else, spend fun time with your partner or child or friend. This will place you back in the present quicker than anything else and put you in a positive mindset.

- Importantly, meditate in your own time, and in a manner that completely suits you. Walk, sit in silence, listen to music, have "you-time" for five, ten, twenty minutes a day or night. Become immersed in the moment, whatever it may be: gardening, walking along the coast, walking a mountain trail, or spending a few valuable moments cocooned in your car listening to the rain or enjoying the sun on your face. At these times, take a moment or two to appreciate what you have in your life right now!

- Finally, make new habits—start and end your day with a few moments of gratitude. Reflect on people and happenings within the day that gave you peace of mind or joyful feelings, a sense of being loved, an inner confidence … a moment that gave you some hope, inner strength, or a sense that everything would be okay. Recognizing these moments as often as you can will create exponential changes in your life.

The more you practice these simple exercises, the more you will benefit.

The ego is so strong in us that it easily tricks us into a false belief that we are being generous and loving when our actions, thoughts, and words are anything but. We so easily react to others and for the most part cannot see our behaviors and reactions until we become aware of their effects and impacts on other people, and as a consequence ourselves. When we see the effects on others or feel the effects within ourselves … we are then able to observe more clearly our thoughts, words, and actions, assess them, and learn what truly makes a difference.

"Unease" is directly caused by the separation we feel from others. This unease gets played out over and over until we take notice, take responsibility for our thoughts, words, and actions, and make the decision to change them.

Hiding behind your finger cannot help you. Vigilance and constant application, until we learn the signals that show us our true path, are so important. We must not decide, after seeing the signal for one moment, to look no further because it's too hard, or have so little faith that we give up without letting our vigilance show us the benefits. This is why we often give up on our path to consciously creating the life we desire most (that is, creating real and lasting change for the better) ... and return to our controlling or demanding habits, fighting every step of the way.

We all love the idea of the law of attraction ... we have heard of its euphoric effects, and we deeply desire the knowledge of how to create them—but what time do we allocate to embracing this *readily available* creative power? In many cases we give ourselves "no time" and "no space" to do so.

Disgruntled by our efforts and our desire for change, which doesn't seem to happen just as we'd wish, we often just give up. We revert to old ways of behaving, thinking, and acting. But we must persist! Persist, and persist; don't let the ego beat you ... we must give our distorted perceptions space (through reflection) so our fears can dissipate. We need to show ourselves a little patience (nurturing the wounded ego-self) to see a different reality unfold and materialize ... and if we do, it will! Patience and persistence are paramount.

We must learn the difference between creating the reality we most desire and manifesting the reality that we thoughtlessly act out. We learn this by doing the following:

- Identifying the truth of our past. Ask yourself, what happened to you? Can you talk it over or write it down? Perhaps seek out professional help if you feel you can invest that time and money in yourself.

- Having the courage to face the past and finding the courage to forgive it. And everything within it.

- Being grateful for the people and things we have in our lives and reminding ourselves of them constantly. Apply gratitude to your life in abundance!

We control, resist, and struggle because of our needy attachments—thoughtless in our every action. To feel a sense of worth or acceptance, we believe, we must fight and resist the many life challenges we have self-manifested. We were taught that life doesn't come easy. We believe in the illusion we learned from others and comply with their lessons ever so perfectly. In the absence of a better way, we hang on to our old ways—we hang on ever so tightly, believing them to be our only chance of freedom.

We must start to ask the relevant questions of ourselves—not in harmful ways, but rather in consoling, nurturing ways, if we want peace, tranquility, and joy in our lives. The secrets lie within our past, and it is our past that we must find the courage to face.

We rely on a life that revolves around self-meaning (ego) ... with little to no faith in life or the universal law of attraction. Many of us lack faith in any higher power, or our own true power ... feeling only fleeting instances of inner Self-trust and guidance.

Our inner Self was created from a loving, omnipotent energy. When we create naturally and purposefully, this allows us to give and receive love effortlessly. Through this expression of love, we create more of it ... what we give is returned in kind ... This is the law of attraction. Our separation from Self, others, or our higher power causes us fear and anxiety because we separate from who we truly are and the purpose through which we were created.

Separation defies everything that we know deep within to be real. To trust this one statement is to begin real and measurable change. Express love and we will see the benefit ... we just need to learn what love actually means. Not shallow love, or limited love, but love from a wholly loving Self. We are not separate and unloving by nature ... and that is why we instinctively know that when we feel separated from anyone else ... we feel unease or worse.

The only place where blind faith is needed, therefore, is in our ability to *start* change. The truth is that something good will inevitably occur from our efforts. It is witnessing change, seeing it and feeling its effects, that gives us the inner strength and power to continue! We aren't being asked to maintain *blind* faith for more than an instant ... we will just need it to get started!

The Truth Found in Meditation

As we practice meditation, uneasy and uncomfortable thoughts will become more and more frequent, simply because the ego we created is highly defensive of our existing reality—the need to be right, the need to justify our actions, the fear of trusting and letting go.

A moment of silence within will bring negative thoughts into conscious awareness. These thoughts may have been repressed or suppressed for a very long time—this is why it is essential to practice meditation for short periods each day.

In time, you will recognize the thoughts and, in so doing, the origin of these thoughts (but only when you're ready to face them). For some, like me, facing them requires professional assistance. Do not be afraid to seek it out if your trauma was significant and you know you need support.

Once we learn to face the reasoning behind our thoughts and how they originated, we have choices. We have the choice to accept them as a life journey with no other emphasis, forgive ourselves for carrying these lessons for so long, forgive those we have held responsible, release these past thoughts, and thereby allow ourselves the ability to live in the present.

EXERCISE
A Simple Exercise in Meditation

- Sit quietly, and breathe deeply into the diaphragm by extending the stomach muscles as you breathe in and slowly breathe out until the breath is all but depleted.

- Repeat the process at least six to eight times.

- Sit quietly, with your back straight and upright, and let your mind wander to all the sounds around you.

- As thoughts appear, simply let them go; they will return if you need them to, so let the mind simply let go and return your focus to the sounds around you.

- Continue to sit quietly for at least ten minutes.

Exercise continues on next page

Exercise continued

No matter how disturbed your thoughts are, you will gain benefits. This moment in Self is invaluable.

Try to get into the daily habit of meditation—in a world that appears mad by design, it is a wonderful lifeline and process of restful awakening.

The only element of blind faith you need is to *start*, trusting that you really are more than you give yourself credit for at times. Know that unease is part and parcel of the process of undoing past beliefs—an essential prerequisite for a healthy mind.

- BE WILLING: If we desire peace and love to flourish in our life we cannot just sit back and remain ignorant of our thoughts, feelings, and behaviors. Not recognizing our truths, or the reasoning behind our distorted beliefs, means we will carry the pain and unease of our past and our ignorance well into old age—fixated on controlling, manipulating, attacking, defending, or reacting rather than allowing life to flow effortlessly. Ultimately, that control we hang on to will drive us insane.

- LOOK INWARD: We must look inward, not outward, for our sense of right or wrong—and we will know it from the feelings that follow. This is inner Self-trust ... looking inward, becoming aware through each physical signal such as uneasiness, hurt, or emotional pain, and thereafter trusting instinctively and having the courage to follow our convictions and change.

- BE POSITIVE: Be positive even if things seem not to be going your way just now. Positive thoughts are in a sense a blind faith. Try to maintain it and observe the outcomes.

- BE GRATEFUL: Feeling grateful for what you have in your life, rather than resentful over what you don't have, will help greatly. Know that everything that has occurred in your life had a divine purpose and that purpose was to lead you through your spiritual/physical evolution. Start and end your day with a few short minutes of gratitude.

- MEDITATE: Meditate each day for a short while as a practice in rest and awareness.

- REMEMBER LIFE HAS MEANING: Know that there is great meaning to life. This encourages us to take part in it rather than remain separate from it, as we have done before! When we know the meaning of life, we will act fearlessly and willingly. To be able to say the simple words "It is a wonderful world" when things look hopeless or desperate is not only courageous but essential. Seeing the glass as half full rather than half empty will help considerably—let's practice! This is what the world needs more of—our positive thoughts, words, and actions that in an instant can begin the process of actual change … the power of conscious creation!

We have come to see our lives and the world around us as everything they are inherently not—fearful, separate, unfair, unequal, lacking compassion and knowledge, and unforgiving. This creates in us our insecurities and "protective" neediness—the thoughts, words, and actions we use to defend our worth. Fear and anxiety manifest our pain and unease, which we then project outward. Is it any wonder we settle deeper into our tunnel vision and refuse to look beyond it!

The truth is that it is love and nurturing we must now offer our ego-self, dropping our guard (in blind faith that more benefits await), taking the first steps to awareness, and remaining quietly and humbly confident in who we are, in the belief that we are being supported and have the power to change our lives for the better. Connectedness to inner Self-love strengthens each time you practice any one of the exercises in this book. Notice which ones work best for you—there is no set program, but rather a process of feeling. The greater your connection, the more joy and peace of mind you will feel.

Our fears will always lead us to experience pain, both directly and indirectly, so it is the fear of life we need to remedy. And it is our choice whether to carry or release that pain. Whether to carry the pain is a choice we must each make … and if we do choose to, we prolong our suffering. The extent of our suffering is therefore a choice. If we are human and on this planet, then pain is not optional—pain is a life given—loss, death, hardships are a part of living in a physical form—but how we manage the pain will determine the quality of our life!

It is as a result of our pain that we will look for alternatives, other possibilities beyond the limits we've put on our life. The choice is ours to make! Run from our past and thereby carry on with the illusion we've created, or choose to face the past so that we can truly move through it—and on to an abundant future? What will you choose?

Let us each make the decision to stand in courage and face the reasoning behind our unease—face it without blame, criticism, or judgment of others. Now, if we do this—if we truly face the unease and do so without blame, criticism, or judgment of others—then who do we have left to look at? The answer is our ego-self! The ego-self we created to protect us … So, regardless of what else you may feel as you venture through this journey, always remain vigilant to ensure you give yourself ample Self-love. Nurture that part of you that was hurt. It is in this clear perception and firm intention to change that real, sustainable, and abundant change begins.

We must face our reality and notice our behaviors and feelings so as to truly love the people and things we have in our life right now! We must appreciate what we have rather than feeling unappreciative of what we do not have—appreciation is the power generator for consciously creating the life we desire!

Look at each gift you have in your life that makes your life a little more blessed, more comfortable—enjoy these gifts and blessings and have the gratitude for them that they deserve. In so doing, we break the pattern of behaviors that have misdirected our thoughts, confused our thinking, and driven our tunnel vision—a vison distortion of our own making.

Each of us will reach a point in life where change is needed. How positive the consequences of that change are will be directly related to the practice we put into making change possible.

Each practice provided in this book supports our spiritual and physical growth.

We are given the tools; we must apply them in our daily lives and reward ourselves with the abundance that awaits.

CHAPTER THREE

SELF-FULFILLED

"A human being is part of the whole, called by us 'Universe,'
a part limited in time and space. He experiences himself, his
thoughts and feelings as something separated from the rest—a
kind of optical delusion of his consciousness. This delusion is
a kind of prison for us, restricting us to our personal desires
and to affection for a few persons nearest to us. Our task
must be to free ourselves from this prison by widening the
circle of compassion to embrace all living creatures and the
whole of nature in its beauty. Nobody is able to achieve this
completely, but the striving for such achievement is in itself
a part of liberation and a foundation for inner security."
Albert Einstein (1879–1955)

What our mind focuses on becomes our reality. Yet overwhelmingly, it is through our innate desire to achieve Self-fulfillment and discover our life's meaning that we attain our primary function—that of reconnecting to our inner Self, regardless of our reality at any given moment.

Self-fulfillment is what we strive toward, either from a distorted reality—an optical illusion within the ego-self that leaves us unfulfilled—or through our instinctive, deeply rooted tendency to pursue meaning and purpose. Ultimately, Self-fulfillment can only ever be achieved through the latter: inner Self-connection and the outward expression of a loving, free Self. Finding this inner Self-connection is a journey—not an immediate destination, as the ego would dictate. In this journey our freedom will be felt, desired, and thereafter embraced, when the mind is free to function as it was intended to.

How do we find Self-fulfillment, if not through seeing clearly, observing our reality, and assessing our thoughts? When we are trapped in the illusionary or misconceived state of mind embedded in our egoic state, the question we must one day ask is … How can our thoughts be wholly real, when our thoughts project our past—that part of us that was wounded and born out of fear? We project fear when our thoughts *do not* move away from believing everything we see—this delusion is a kind of prison, restricting us to our personal bodily desires. Where, then, is our faith in the inner Self?

What is Self? The Self is a mind free of bodily functions and controls, in a highly creative state. It is a Self without limits, highly knowledgeable, and in control.

Because it is without limits, it wholly creates heartfelt desires; because it is knowledge, it knows unequivocally our desires; and being in control, it does not have to *impose* controls. Here the mind is free to create and be itself.

In effect, our thoughts must change from belief in everything we see to thoughtful awareness of everything we feel. Here, change begins.

We are in effect individuals who are part of a greater unity consciousness (the sum of all individuals). We have the power to love, share, and care, yet too often we do not embrace this Self, believing we must control and protect our minute realities and those close to us. But will that thinking ultimately protect us or them? No—and what lessons do we pass on when we limit our reality to such a small sphere?

The ego-self is an unloved and unloving self, regardless of appearances. It does not believe in unity—it was hurt, and seeks rectification and strongly follows the doctrines of "separation and ego- power" (a form of idolization in itself). Its ethos is attack or defend—it needs to protect its idol image—and its outcome is "ultimate failure."

In our egoic state, thoughts are mere perceptions firmly shored up by how much value we place on the image we have created of ourselves. Tell someone they're wrong and see the reaction. Fear will always require defense. But give that same self a small dose of love and the reply varies considerably. Fear-based thoughts are not wholly real, because thoughts from an unloved self are unsure and fickle. No sustainable foundation exists, and it is here that our distorted thinking and poor behaviors lie.

Self-fulfillment is an inner knowing and trust: inner Self-love. Its views don't change because its thoughts do not need to change ... operating from a loving foundation, it does not defend, attack, or control—it just is, observing, accepting, sharing, loving, and guiding in kindness ... with joy and peace of mind each "a constant" when we are held in this state of being.

The pain and fear of an unloved self that we project is, in truth, our "cry for love," producing awkward or unwarranted behaviors that are usually returned in kind, since they are experienced by others as personal attacks. This further frustrates us as we perceive that our reality is invalidated and that life lacks meaning.

We feel hurt and stubbornly hide our disappointment or attack in response. We simply don't know how to adequately express how we feel or how to authentically connect to others. We do not know what love is in our ego-self—we can't possibly—we just *think* we do. Love provides something deeper than words; it puts the mind into its natural state, and in that state it becomes content and fulfilled and shares the gifts of peace and joy. Hiding this truth, though, is all-important—dare we let anyone see we aren't perfect?

Some of our most influential world leaders reflect this all too obviously ... they plainly incite division and hate, and we judge them accordingly, either condemning or glorifying them—our own fears determining which judgment we make. Yet this tough and unloving outward expression stems from their feeling that they are not loved themselves. Their egos dominate, concealing their own fears, and many suffer as a consequence. Just as love circles back on itself, so too does fear, with reality being created from what each mind focuses on.

Everybody wants to be loved, yet we're so afraid to be completely open and vulnerable that the chance is lost in the illusion we create instead.

We live within an unconscious reality (thoughtless, fearful reality) that escalates and becomes more consuming as we grow older. It appears to confirm our long-held belief that "separation" is real—separation belief syndrome is the cause of all our problems. How did we accept this reality? The answer is through hard work— many years of taking on the distorted thinking of others, in layer after layer, and experiencing sufficient trauma to feel we must either sink or swim, fight or flee, attack or defend.

As individuals, we are comforted by the physical norms we grew up with. While the experiences we encounter may be painful, we do very little to recognize our pain and unease until our lives become unmanageable. This often occurs much later in life. Our lives are a reflection of the beliefs we were taught growing up, and we live by them—suppressing and denying our reality, and projecting more of the same. Our world is a clear example of the separation and fear we experience. Yet even though these painful experiences are thoughtless and unloving, thankfully they still have a purpose in the greater plan of life.

Our inner Self is divinely connected to our own spiritual being, which is connected to every other spiritual being—whole, unlimited, unbounded. Self-love is the foundation of our willpower when things just don't seem right. Our darkest days will reveal an "instinct" to search for something inside us—something new, which must be better than what we are experiencing. It is this instinctive Self we need to listen to.

Our quest to evolve spiritually is inherent, a matter of course … and it's determined by how fulfilled we feel … thankfully we have no choice in the matter. It is predetermined by how we were created. However hard we resist, it will be fear that ultimately turns our thinking around to something far greater than we could hide within the limited reality we once created and normalized.

Thankfully, consciousness (the highly intelligent nature of all things) determines the outcome, not us. There is a power that resides in us that is far greater than we are, yet is indivisible from us. We are all a part of the whole—we refer to it as a greater consciousness. But when are we going to accept this? Knowing this is so important to our peace of mind and well-being because in reconnecting we complete two primary life goals: inner Self-validation and discovery of life's meaning. Both strengthen our life purpose and Self-fulfillment.

The lessons we encounter, then live with, and finally look back on and observe are key to the process of trusting there is something greater than the way we think now (our current limited reality). Therefore, at some point the past plays its role—its purpose is to allow us to look back, identify and learn, then forgive, nothing more. Thereafter, the body becomes the instrument of learning as the mind, free of bodily constraints, communicates in loving ways through it … to become aware, to learn, to evolve. Painful, emotionally unhealthy, and unhelpful behaviors are replaced by loving, Self-fulfilling actions.

To know the unlimited potentiality (unity consciousness) we each possess at the core of our being, we need to acquire the tools to connect to it. The paradox of learning something we already know may be bewildering—but remember that the past has played a significant role in our distorted truths. Where we are right now is significant—coming from an unloved, fearful egoic state lacking Self-love, and learning to once again trust the center of our being.

How we think is determined by what we prioritize—we build a hierarchical tree of life. When I was growing up within my family of origin, my own hierarchal tree was somewhat unstable and left me wanting—it gave a distorted view of life:

PAST BELIEFS: A WHOLLY EXTERNALLY FOCUSED MINDSET

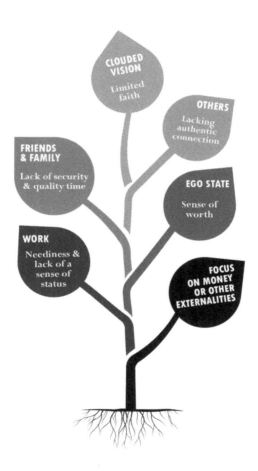

Weak roots, life dependent on external factors, an unreliable guide, creates a constant sense of fear

The difficulty with the belief system in the above diagram was that if the tree was shaken, for example if a partner or friend was destabilized for any one of a myriad of reasons, through poor expressions of love, I had no support to rely on—hence I would desperately defend my position in an effort to feel I was "right."

The two inherent, permanent, and omnipotent kinds of life energy—inner Self-love, and trust in a universal power on which we can rely—were at the bottom of my priority list, and I rarely relied on them apart from sporadically when things just became too exhausting. The effects of having limited faith in Self and Self-love are a lack of fulfillment and ultimately exhaustion—in our ego state we feel like we have little control so we constantly fight to remain in control.

I was closed off to a few square meters of reality—my Alamo. I needed to acquire a reliable and steadfast source of support. A reliable guide to instruct me on my journey ... that wasn't coming from within, unfortunately, but rather from all things outside my ego-self.

Which part of the tree received the light to feed it? Material possession. Surely an unstable basis for any conscious existence or attempt to manifest the best parts of life.

I placed my work, partner, and friends before my own sense of worth because I had very little of it. I put these three aspects of my life on a pedestal, to make it appear to the world that I had succeeded, that I was important. Outer attachments, no matter which ones, were all-important. I completely convinced myself that I was happy and content and that all was perfect. I was living a lie and recreating the same life tree I had been shown in my childhood. I made others important—in hindsight, all for my own sake and sense of self-worth.

If we wish a functional, sustainable, and Self-fulfilling reality to unfold, we must develop the skills to replace our old tree structures. New perceptions gained through our vigilant awareness can help us do so immeasurably. Looking truthfully at the past will bring about this wisdom, and each of us has the power within to access the peace and joy that will inevitably arise from it. As a permanent and reliable structure of universal life support, the tree should look like this:

UPDATED BELIEFS: THE INSIGHT OF TRUTH AND WISDOM

CLARITY
In life

WORK
A passion for doing

OTHERS
Authentic connections

FRIENDS & FAMILY
Happiness & joy

SELF LOVE
Inner Self-love & trust become your guide

FAITH
A powerful belief in a higher purpose

Deeply rooted in life, solid foundation and strong growth, a sustainable and wholly reliable Self-guide: a prerequisite of joy and peace

By contrast, in this tree life exists through you. You, and the universe around you. In truth, they are one and the same. You are your mentor … Why? Because you/we are all part of the whole of it! This hierarchal tree does not mean we can't have material possessions or the drive to fulfill our desires, in any form that doesn't hurt others, but if the tree is shaken, we rely solely on Self for answers—a Self that categorically knows the answers to life, our journey, and our purpose. It is in accepting this journey that our faith strengthens, as we begin to see real, wonderful, and tangible change.

There is an omnipotent energy within our universe that will never abandon you. (As we have seen, however, it can be blocked by the fear-based thought processes generated by past trauma.) This lies in the faith and belief (in the unseen) we need to kick-start our relationship with Self—this faith in life itself that we can each access as a means of universal support. What would you say if you knew it was *you* who had abandoned *it*? Would you look for ways to reconnect? You probably would, and the proof would not leave you blind for long, as you would witness immediate benefits through the mere willingness to do so.

We need faith to start—call it a blind faith for now, but with a genuine intent; soon, you will see and feel the realization of your deepest desires. This early evidence of the many benefits of your "willingness to reconnect" will fortify your inner belief and trust, which over time will become unshakeable.

When we connect to Self, we sense something beyond the limited understanding we've known for so long. It is in fact a universal omnipotent energy that awaits our willingness—when the mind connects to it, peace will reside within. We will feel Self-love and acquire an instant "knowing" that it is real.

These feelings and emotions will be enough to plant the seed and the willingness to learn more. And that is all we need … *the seed capital.*

At the age of fourteen I abandoned God, religion, and faith because I thought I was abandoned. Anxiety was as much a part of my life as breathing. How could there be a God while I lived in so much fear, suffered so many social phobias and addictions? Religion could not help me—in fact, it made me feel worse. According to the faith in which I was raised I would have been described as a sinner, and my options were to repent or suffer retribution … Yet even if I wanted to, how could I repent if I didn't have the means? I was too disconnected from my inner Self. Forgiveness? I had too much blame.

We live in ways that cause us to feel shame and guilt, and many of us are looked on as unforgivable souls. Or people who need pity and prayer. This is not mentorship; it is manipulation and control that takes away our own confidence in Self.

Once we develop the skill for trusting in Self, we develop the skill to accept life, including all our past misperceptions and illusionary, fearful beliefs, and learn by them instead. We learn to think without fear, take more chances (because we took that important first step of taking the first chance)—and feel differently. We give our Self a chance to live with renewed vigor—freely and more passionately in the present. The mind, remember, will always take the path of least resistance. Show it love over fear and it will follow love.

It is when we take chances that the universe supports our willingness! Free of the need for validation or approval by anyone but Self, our lives open up to many possibilities. The mind is free, so the body follows. True creation is allowed to function.

What I came to realize was that the greatest fight was with myself (ego-self)—I tried to create the so-called perfect reality ... But it was not perfect—I only believed it was. I lived in denial and had no mentor to speak of. Who could be my mentor, other than the fears I carried?

How do we connect to the Self ... and this unity consciousness?

- First, we must FEEL what it is we feel. When searching for peace in our lives, it is not appropriate to deny our feelings. Feeling is the conduit to the soul and guides us to our instinctive knowing.

  ◦ Remember, the body/mind reacts but the soul/mind *creates* ... the latter is what we are attempting to relearn—in order to consciously create whatever we desire through a mind–soul connection.

  ◦ When we express how we feel, we soon observe our reality. Are we experiencing a mind–body union (unease), or mind–soul union (peace and harmony)?

- Second, when we become aware of any challenging behavior we are displaying, we must notice at some level the unease that prompts it. Once again, this is a signal to identify with our feelings. To face the TRUTH of why we feel the way we do.

There are many telltale behaviors we can become aware of—let me give you some examples of easy-to-see signs:

- Do you often find you're angry?

- Are you unable to stop thinking?

- Do you make no time for loved ones, and always make excuses?

- Do you lack gratitude in your life or have difficulties expressing gratitude?

- Do you lack life balance—the balance between family, work, and play?

- Are you unable to see the joy in life—in the people and the simple things that surround you—and instead see life as a chore or burden?

- Do you suffer from stress and complain about it?

- Do you find yourself needing to control every aspect of your life—criticize, judge, opinionate, blame?

- Do you have trouble listening to others?

- Are you unable to sit quietly and calmly without feeling restless or needing to do something/anything instead?

- Do you wake up early in the morning with an overactive mind?

- Do you easily become attached to people and things from a need to possess, control, or manipulate?

- ◦ Do you go into your shell, afraid to express your needs and wants?

- ◦ Do you do what others would have you do, to keep the peace?

- ◦ Do you accept the poor behaviors of others at the expense of your own well-being?

If you find it difficult to feel or identify your true feelings, simply observe your behaviors. After observing your behaviors, you can then ask yourself, "How am I feeling?" Keep trying until you master the art of asking the question and answering it honestly!

- Third, we must take time in the stillness and silence of Self to hear what it is we truly need. Become AWARE of your unease or other feelings. To start with, practice meditation for just a few minutes a day—you will begin to trust in your Self.

- Finally, be VIGILANT in identifying your feelings and behaviors throughout the day. In time, this will lead you to discover the thoughts behind them … and in knowing your thoughts, you begin to take back control, *real* control, of your life—you begin to change the thoughts that cause your unease and replace it with a sense of peacefulness.

  Start the day … ask the question, "How do I feel right now?" Sit with Self in a few moments of silence, and become consciously aware of what it is you feel.

  End the day with the same process and do a mental stocktake of how the day went and how it could have gone better.

  CONSCIOUS AWARENESS + FEELING = SOUL CONNECTION

Once we identify the unease we feel, we can make a conscious choice to change. Change the thought behind the unease, and the unease dissipates. Once you know what it is you feel, you can then ask another question of yourself: "*Why* am I feeling like this?" It is then that you can make the conscious choice to change. Or not!

Change the feeling—change the behavior. Change behavior— change reality. You won't change if you don't know what you're feeling, and why!

You may be thinking, "I can't just make the decision to do so, just like that" ...

Imagine a friend has said something unexpectedly that hurt you. They may have not said it in malice but, rather, to make themselves stand out from the crowd ... but you perceive it as fun at your expense. Your resentment could lead you to reply angrily, or worse. If you knew the reasoning behind your friend's hurtful comment, you could make a conscious choice to talk it over and resolve how you feel. Perhaps they misunderstood you. How often does this play out? How often does it block our peace of mind? Taking the responsible action of talking things through would free your mind and unburden you of the many difficult thoughts and processes that inevitably follow these interludes.

Our fearful self lives by the slogan "I won't tell you what I think and feel because I'm afraid of what you may think and feel" ... and as a consequence, unresolved issues create an unpleasant reality that we can easily fixate on. Present moments lost to past demands!

We have learned not to trust love; we have learned not to express our true Self. We have been hurt by those who said they loved us. We have become disillusioned with what we were taught. We have all learned to question love.

Because we have been conditioned to hide our feelings, we simply refuse to be aware of how we feel—if we knew what we felt, then we would understand the need to change! Often, we feel anxious, uneasy, alone, sad, overly committed, bored, unsatisfied, unappreciative, hurt, resentful, and fearful of life. Overthinking it at every turn. Most of us live in a constant state of fear and anxiety and we cope by normalizing this state of being. Avoiding our feelings is at pandemic levels. How do we find Self-fulfillment if we don't know what it is we feel, or why?

It is possible to give life real meaning if we look at it in a most logical way. There must be more to life than to be born, live for eighty or ninety years (if we're lucky!), and then die. Surely, given the wonders of nature and this magnificent universe that exists in perfect synchronicity, there must be a logical and divine purpose to our being here.

Perhaps our purpose is to experience every aspect of the lives we live, experience the fears within those lives, and thereby, at a certain point in time, choose to look inward, not outward, for answers. The only sustainable foundation is to find more love—fear's opposite number.

What would make your physical journey purposeful, hopeful, and trusting, and thus more enjoyable, peaceful, and loving? Recognition of the importance of your journey and your divine purpose. Too many of us have lost faith in life, and rarely feel it has a true purpose regardless of how much we acquire materially.

Our lesson and purpose within our short lifespan is to know the opposite of love, through the fear we learn so well, and thereby desire to create greater love—in this knowledge lies our spiritual/physical evolution. Ultimately, this is our goal and our path to a fulfilled life. Trust and faith will create an abundant life no matter how little we believe this in this moment. Love *must* create a more fulfilled and abundant life. We are on a journey to find this out, and the sooner we embrace it the sooner we will discover the truth.

It would defy logic and reason if we were to assume that we were bigger than the ultimate power of all there is. To believe in separation is to assume that the greatest power is less than perfect. Our higher power is the basis of perfection—it is gentle, nurturing, all-loving, complete, and whole. How could it be anything else? The universe is all there is and more. It is loving, divine, potent energy in perpetual motion. Pure conscious energy, forever expanding in perpetual motion that exists without fear.

It is this energy that resides in each of us; we are as much a part of it as anything in existence—it expands as we create more love within it.

Remember, only fear breaks things apart, dividing, making separation possible—the physical world as we experience it is our best example.

Fear cannot exist outside our physical reality; if it did, then all that we know in our universe could not exist.

We go through most of life not even realizing there is an alternative to the distorted and painful reality we live with each day.

We fail to see the signs within our thoughts or behaviors and too often normalize our feelings of unease. In a thoughtless state of ignorance we do not realize that those who taught us lessons of separation and fear taught us what they learned themselves. Forgiveness becomes near impossible.

We believe that we can rid ourselves of unease by resisting and controlling life, rather than accepting it—resistance is what we witness each and every day. We witness more pain in the world, and dwell in the pain and suffering it offers, if only at a subliminal level. The world we see confirms our fears and our distorted belief in an unfulfilling world. In the absence of awareness, we seem quite willing to live with our unease—preferring this ignorant reality to facing the truth of our lives and making changes that can offer us life's abundance. Our ignorance has become what we know to be real, and yet it is anything other than real—it is all in our head. The lessons of fear taught to us remain embedded in our minds and tell us that it is by resisting life that we will be saved from our unease— hence our need to control and manipulate each and every aspect of our lives.

We choose to experience more of the same pain we have come to believe to be part and parcel of life rather than look for an alternative path—we look, finally, only when our own life crumbles in front of us, providing the final proof that the ego-self couldn't save us after all! ... And that perhaps we do actually need to question the reality that we have believed in for so long. It is only when the illusion of our ego-self is shattered that we are forced to feel what it is we truly feel! It is then we may ask the question we need to ask: "Is there a better way?"

The really good news for us is that no matter what decision we make, we will advance spiritually, and for this reason no decision is a wrong one!

Once we realize that there is no wrongdoing, we can forgive ourselves for the hurt we have allowed ourselves to experience. When we forgive self, we can forgive others—often our grievances against others are nothing more than an unforgiven self.

If there are aspects of someone else over which you hold grievances, then look at yourself and ask, "Are they in fact grievances against my ego-self, and which part of myself have I still not forgiven?"

We may perceive that there is no part of self that needs our forgiveness—until we muster the courage required to recognize it. It is a choice for our own betterment and freedom, similar to what we may have witnessed in others who have suffered a great deal and who have every reason to hold on to grievances but ultimately display forgiveness.

In true spiritual terms, the body is an instrument of learning and helps us evolve by experiencing fear, and, through knowing fear so intimately, learn the many aspects of love—caring, sharing, oneness, openness, laughter, spontaneity, joy, peace, bliss, and so much more.

How would we value these attributes of love, if we did not experience its opposite—carelessness, greed, separation, sadness, loneliness, grief, anger, or anxiety? We have all heard the saying "love has no opposite," and to know this we must first learn to recognize fear. We learn to recognize it … and then, dutifully, release it.

We use the body to learn this lesson of opposites and then revel in the joys of knowing when we reconnect to Self. As we have discussed previously, learning who we are in truth, and understanding that who we are is in fact the opposite of the body that represents us, is the purpose that gives our lives incredible meaning—we are each the mind that lies within us, as it does within every living thing in existence, divinely created as part of the one greater Self.

Therefore, to know this perfection we must experience imperfection. In physical form, we are each imperfectly perfect at doing that.

It is perfectly okay to be imperfect—it is why we are here!

So let's face our imperfection openly and honestly, without shame or guilt, for it is through imperfection that we evolve!

We have kept secrets all our life from fear of being ridiculed, abandoned, criticized, and judged. Too often our family of origin taught us the lesson of keeping secrets from their own experiences, passed on to them by previous generations—the same teachings passed down throughout generations and seen clearly within society, schools, political systems, and religious denominations. Our world teaches fear—whether the goal is to control or manipulate, it produces a never-ending cycle of our own egos perpetuating more fear. Our families, our institutions, and the societies in which we live taught us to say nothing, to deny our truths and defend our fears.

As we grew up, often our feelings didn't matter, or mattered only because they mattered to someone who needed our feelings, thoughts, and words to validate *them*! So ultimately, did our feelings really matter? Such was the control others had over us, and we learned to suppress our true feelings as a consequence.

We create another self—our adapted ego-self—to portray a stronger "me," an unaffected, untouchable, suspicious, acceptable "me"—or we become victims—the manipulative, calculating other "me," to get our needs and wants met. These are the personalities we show to the world, rather than the loving, vulnerable self we were born as, and the world shows our fearful self back to us—it is what we bring about through the law of attraction.

In this false perception of life, life appears to lack love and our perceptions become further distorted—yet all any of us is ever calling for is two things: love and acceptance. Love and acceptance are what we desire, above all else!

Remember, life is exactly how it is intended to be—we experience fear and, as we manifest more of it, ultimately our life will become unmanageable and we will look for alternatives. The timing of our decision to look for alternatives is entirely up to each of us.

Once our thoughtlessness manifests the necessary crisis in our life, or our pain becomes unmanageable, "our path to peace" will immediately come to mind. Why? It is our inner core knowing—our return to who we are—that Self is found in the moment of our choosing—Self is constantly awaiting our awareness and asking to return. And the reason we become aware is because pain shatters the defense mechanism of the ego and the controlling aspect of this ego-self—we render it immobile by our questioning of our fear and the distorted reality, and we see that it has ultimately delivered nothing of substance—facing truth in present-moment awareness!

The ego loses its power once the vulnerable, open, and nurturing inner you is made aware. In the light of our consciousness (present-moment awareness), fear (ego) loses its power. When the disconnection between mind and body occurs, which it will always do when the ego mind has been shattered, the mind immediately links back to its true source—the spirit or Self—and it will disengage from the body, knowing that the body has no power over it. Our mind turns back to the place it knows, trusts deeply, and relies on—its home—the inner Self looking inward ... no longer outward ... for the answers to life.

How can we instantly connect to our "instinctive" inner Self?
Feeling what you truly feel is the starting point!

Your immediate feelings, if given the chance, will guide you away from pain or unease to the possibility of another reality within the safety and love of your inner Self.

Connecting to Self can *instantly* overcome any fear you hold, when you learn how ... And it is not hard: we only perceive this task to be hard because of our fixed and uncompromising ego beliefs. Becoming willing to try is the hardest part; then it gets easier, because we feel in Self-connection a gentle connectedness to something far greater—we feel more love, a certain confidence, and support.

We are created in love and will return to love as a natural consequence of the painful experiences we have lived with. Our return to love, at the moment of our choosing to do so, is an inherent gift of our spiritually created form.

The world we see is hurting, and we are hurting each other in intolerable ways. We can choose to find peace, love, and joy in our life by making a conscious decision to do so ... and in the moment we do, we will experience Self-fulfillment.

The choice is for each of us to make.

CHAPTER FOUR

OVERZEALOUSNESS

"Life shrinks or expands in proportion to one's courage."
Anaïs Nin

Each attribute, characteristic, or condition examined within these chapters exists merely to create awareness. Nothing should be looked at as bad or good … just purely looked at, at face value. Looked at so that a heightened awareness plays wicketkeeper in your life and allows you a much-needed breather so you can recognize where you are and recoup, and thereby provide you with choices. Choices that will play an inspiring and powerful role in your life.

What is Overzealousness?

In the simplest terms, it is the outcome of a dogged and driven mind. When we hold fear of any kind within us, our vision gets narrower and less clear. As a result, we engage in overly passionate thoughts or behaviors to fix the discomfort we feel.

We do not recognize our behaviors for what they are, as our focused, tunneled attention (tunnel vision) leaves no room for common sense or reasoning, or for the mind to discover or even consider other possibilities. Tunnel vision means wearing blinders that focus energy on a desired outcome, and overzealousness is what results from this ultra-focused, limited view.

It can be argued quite easily that overzealous behaviors and tunnel vision both have benefits, and it can be true, depending on mindset and the outcome desired at the time. A limited understanding of what brings happiness may best be served by these attributes; however, we must ask ourselves, "How sustainable are the outcomes?"

While short-term gain is something we often obsess over, it is frequently followed by a sense of loss. Hence, we take a journey to uncover certain truths.

Think of a workaholic—you may hear of many successes in some aspects of their life, and yet so many personal failures in other areas. Among the most obvious examples are those personalities with high public profiles, be they famous actors, singers, or entrepreneurs, whose success impacts negatively on their personal lives.

The trash magazines are full of it, and we often get relief from reading them, as if doing so allows us to believe that we are not alone. Observing this truth behind the egoic state allows a moment of reprieve for each of us to just take a short breath and ask, "Am I going about this the right way?"

Living life is about a passion for doing; passion exists in the present moment. When our behaviors exceed a passion for doing (when we become overzealous), we need to ask ourselves why. If we don't, then ultimately the behaviors will take us to a point where we have little choice but to question our reality.

Have you ever broken up a relationship and just couldn't let it go, making the acrimony between you and your partner significantly worse, with many outside the relationship suffering worse still?

Ever lost a business deal and found yourself on the phone, constantly complaining, blaming, or incessantly wondering how or why?

Has a family member, friend, or colleague said or done things that upset you and you find yourself consumed by it and constantly verbalizing or internalizing what you can or can't do about it?

Have you ever looked back on a situation where, if you had handled your overzealous behaviors differently, you might have landed in a completely different place?

Conflicts form internally, then are projected externally, as we seek a sustainable outcome from a driven focus, to meet an insatiable need to win life's perceived psychological battles.

This behavior can be observed in others, and thereafter translated by a different form of seeing (see my book *Silent*—hear with your eyes, see with your ears).

We must all learn to see less and learn more.

Due to the emotional and physical energy we project in an egoic state, we have little access to mindful thinking or rest to replenish our energy. When we are over-passionate about anything, balance is lost; too much energy goes in one direction—outward—and this is best described as living with fear and anxiety and learning to normalize it.

Looking for like-minded others to confirm our position, status, or opinions is an important aspect of overzealous behavior. It may lead to an energetic outer persona, and inward feelings of depression while the behavior itself drives the unsuspecting mind to perform on cue. This will continue as long as we hold on to any trace of a poor perception. No reprieve is possible until a result is obtained in one's own favor, or at the point when our efforts fail to provide adequate answers to the fear we feel and the body becomes exhausted. It is at this point, however, that the mind usually separates from obsessive body-identification and turns to reasoning to find an alternative solution.

The challenge with overzealous behavior is that society has come to normalize, approve of, or even glorify it. The overzealous are often viewed by others as survivors, personalities, people who are not afraid of life, who are adventurous, dogged, determined … but the truth is that, as with all egoic traits, fear is the motivation.

Overzealousness often prevents us from just sitting quietly and being comfortable within Self or feeling peace of mind on a regular basis. It acts on the unease or fear we feel over an outward perception and is in turn projected outward … It is the need to control every aspect of our life, with little to no faith save in the effort we apply to life ourselves. Over time, what undermines these fixed positions is the unrealized outcomes or feelings of dissatisfaction that our efforts produce, and behaviors that don't serve us well long term … overwork, food issues, alcohol and drug use, anger and readiness to react, the constant need to defend positions, addictions, constant anxiety, health issues, and living as if on a roller coaster, experiencing many highs and lows. The list goes on, and is all too easily normalized.

When we're being overzealous, an authentic connection to life and others is lost to the pursuit of *any* connection to fill the gaps—self-interest becomes neediness—the need to overcome this sense of loss. Life lacks meaning and we experience only fleeting moments of happiness—bubbles of happiness that we cling to but which easily pop. In this state, we can't recognize the importance of authentic connection to Self or others—a connection that can turn a bubble into a hot air balloon to sail above our earthly concerns.

Due to the excessive self-interest of the ego-self, we perceive that "we give more than we get," and hide our true feelings, so any expression of self is limited to a poor perception of how we see ourselves. In this sense this condition of self-interest further detracts from authentic and sustainable communication with others—it does little to inspire healthy communication long term, and most relationships we participate in are fickle at best.

Living life to the fullest means finding our path to peace of mind. Peace of mind can only be found with an authentic, loving connection to others. To recap—we are individual consciousnesses forming part of a whole consciousness. That is why the only outcome that ultimately and consistently satisfies our Self is when we unite as a whole—it is what we innately know and desire. Our ability to authentically connect is vital for our well-being and joy.

If you have doubts, then ask yourself this: "Why are you able to find solace and solitude even when the path you have been on has relentlessly failed to provide you with the answers you were searching for?" Often, we stand steadfast in our beliefs, and find like-minded others to support our views, yet still things don't feel right. If you took all the "right" actions, which the overzealous mind requires, yet still did not achieve the best possible outcome, instead repeating the same old thoughts and behaviors over and over—who other than *you* can make you feel better, and who other than *you* leads you to reflect that maybe there is another way? The truth can only be that an inner knowing must be guiding you.

The inner Self is the only means of sustaining the best outcome— we must block the external noise and start listening.

Zest for Life vs. Overzealous Living

Zest for life is a passion for life—a confidence gained through knowledge. Knowledge acquired through understanding one's life experiences and applying reasoning and truth to them in order to balance life and know what is most important in living it.

Zest for life gives life meaning and purpose. It is living in the present, communicating authentically, sharing, and doing things that bring the greatest joy. Zest, I have come to realize, is having a passion for being alive, and viewing life as a gift, not a burden— taking responsibility by looking at situations honestly, then looking inwardly for answers.

Zest involves a positive outlook on life—not being scarred by judgments or criticisms but merely observing and passionately acting on them in the confidence that any action will bring a desired response—not just to ourselves but also to others. It is very much aligned with present-moment thinking, deeply engrained in gratitude and appreciation, and immensely enjoyed because a zestful life seems to serve rather than block our respective paths. In a state of present-moment-ness, our thoughts are based in reality and free of the conditioned responses we often employ when attempting to merely survive or to gain something. Zest starts with observing life before responding, and giving the mind time to reason out any reply. When we learn to view life inwardly and then look outward, rather than looking outward before reacting inwardly, our responses produce results we may physically see that build our faith and confidence in the process of life. Life becomes less fearful and many times more hopeful and rewarding.

By contrast, overzealousness is a set of behaviors sourced from a completely different mindset. Its motivation is fear and it operates on the basis of our past experiences with limited understanding or willingness to look beyond them. It's evident that our over-passionate doing is really more a need to deny our true feelings, and to justify any negative thoughts and behaviors that follow.

Overzealousness describes the choice to pursue a lifestyle in which we hope to excel, but the results reveal, if observed correctly, that it is more about a game of survival … We have a limited understanding of the manner in which we live life and what our priorities really are.

Once we begin to accept that maybe there is more to life, we can start to ask relevant questions that will lead us to be more acutely aware of the limitations our behaviors place on our lives.

Peace of mind derives its power from gratitude, love, and acceptance and builds faith that we are universally supported. "Unity consciousness" is not just words on paper but understood as if we had always known it as part and parcel of our make-up. Gratitude, love, and acceptance come about when we value peace of mind above all else.

Physical and spiritual harmony is something we feel in the body. In fact, it is the body's purpose to feel this. Just as the fear we carry creates unease and pain in the body, our spiritual and physical harmony creates peace and joy.

While we may often think that we are living life, even believing "I'm really living life" or "I'm living the dream," these thoughts can obscure the truth that we are, in fact, missing out on life completely! Being overly zealous is not right or wrong; it's merely a distortion of our thinking process at a point in time. We should not condemn ourselves for this but realize that each experience to this point in our life is nothing other than a part of our life journey. In fact, it's part of our life purpose. It is our purpose to experience all manner of things, to learn, grow wiser, and evolve in order to find the peace, joy, and love we each wholly deserve.

We have become masters of suppression and denial. Our behaviors can show us clearly whether we are denying ourselves the opportunity to live life in the manner we would most enjoy. Overzealous behaviors throw us out of equilibrium and then give way to further imbalance and distortion. Drama and conflict are not aspects of an authentic life: they are among the delusions we generate in the absence of life balance. Conversely, physical and spiritual harmony enables us to accept life, no matter what happens, and know that there is a greater plan to everything we experience. We literally view life internally and do not rely on it externally. Through this alone, our personality and outlook change immeasurably.

Without meaning and purpose in life, we are continually looking for them! And how do we find meaning and purpose? *The answer is as simple as this: we can feel peace and joy in the things we do! In fact, we find consistency between our thoughts, words, and actions.* When we experience the impact of these loving attributes on our life, they become deeply desirable to us. Our desires change our focus.

Let's look at how overzealous behavior and thoughts cause us to miss out on life. It may be that our friendships or romances don't work out as planned, or that the love we hoped to experience in these relationships is diminished by misunderstandings that cause blame, arguments, judgments, and criticisms.

We often take our feelings of discontent into our personal lives. And into our workplaces, just the same. Early in my career, I employed thirty or so people in one of my companies. I noticed that when the business was small everyone felt a connection. As the business grew, however, so did the level of people's aggravation. People who had been in the business since its inception obviously felt less loved, as they received less attention. There were new personalities to compete with, and new staff needed training.

Drama and conflict would start. The behaviors senior staff adopted to get attention could be viewed as overzealousness. They could be compared with rowing a boat continuously against a current—it stopped many of them from achieving their full potential or expressing their full capabilities. In some cases, their income suffered, and they felt even more stressed when blame became part of their mindset. They rowed harder and harder until they were exhausted. They either gave up and moved on, or stayed put and regressed, repeating the same process all over again ... many times!

When we do not wish to face the truth behind our reality, the way we live, we keep doing the same things over and over hoping for a different outcome. We all seem to be looking for this different outcome—a brighter now or a better future. But in the process of pursuing it, our overzealousness means we miss our zest for life.

For as long as I could remember, I spent my days planning for the future. In hindsight, I now know that my every thought was determined by my past experiences. When my expectations of others weren't met, I would easily react, over-opinionate, or try to control the outcome in some way. How easy it was to judge, criticize, or expect more when the state of play demanded a win! This tendency could strain my relationships, particularly with those closest to me. They too felt they enjoyed little quality time or balance. However, my behaviors went on, as they always had ... in my mind, there was everything to play for and too much to lose ... change wasn't an option, nor was looking at the "why" behind it all.

The pressure on the people in my life to give up on having their true needs and wants met was never relieved. Thus, more often than not my relationships imploded. In the process, I lost what I did not wish to lose.

I had a completely distorted vision of how life should really be. For me, feeling loved and accepted meant succeeding at overzealous pursuits. The drama became my norm. Long-held distorted principles became my primary motivation for communication. I believed I was the glue in other people's lives, as if I knew better. I was living out a dream of success, doing anything I could to escape my past, obscuring my hidden feelings of loneliness (which I felt no matter who was in my life), and acting out from a lack of self-worth. It was all-important to deny I had a problem. In other words, I was valuing what was, in truth, valueless!

What I am now certain of is that many people live this type of life. Many of us live our lives manipulating others and comparing ourselves to others, unhappy with what we have and wanting what others have. We control others to get a desired outcome, resist others who question us, fight for what at the time we think we need, all in order to find happiness and abundance. Abundance we want even without knowing, from an ego mindset, what abundance is.

Abundance could be described in many ways. As I have come to understand it, it is *the love and acceptance we share from a liberated mindset, at peace with the experiences we project into a zestful life through our thoughts, words, and actions.*

However we have lived life, we aren't by any means bad; we may simply have been misguided by past beliefs, and the limitations these past beliefs caused have led us to search endlessly for something to rescue us. To the ego mind, no matter what we have, enough will never be enough.

Being overzealous will easily manifest as shallow love—an expression of an unloved self, born from tunnel vision, it will manifest highs and lows and unresolved outcomes, and these unresolved issues will leave us feeling less than fulfilled and lacking in love.

A Sense of Lack

The idea of "lack" implies that we would be better off if we had something more tangible in our lives, rather than simply being comforted by who we are, or what we have in this moment, or what we are capable of—if we didn't need *more* to feel wealthy, grateful, and abundant.

If we felt confident and knowledgeable, and had a real sense of self-worth, we would think anything was possible and be satisfied with our approach to life—as if we had an inner knowledge of what to do in any situation; by definition, we wouldn't have any needs outside of ourselves.

With inner Self-connection, there is no sense of lack or loss. This is probably the greatest and most desirable aspect of inner Self-connection. Life becomes an expression of our true Self, with peace and joy the outcome. We know what to say and do because our thoughts come from a wholly trusted place. Life can still challenge us, but our reactions are very different.

Overzealous behavior obscures this possibility; often, the overexertion that stems from a poor sense of self-worth can lead to a poor outcome. We are too busy cleaning up the unresolved issues left behind—unresolved arguments with partners or colleagues, deadlines missed, opportunities lost, the drama caused by overthinking drama. If things don't feel right, it's probably because they *aren't* right. It is not about right and wrong—it's about our finding out … what brings us peace and joy, vs. the constant anxiousness and concern that do not?

The reason we do not go within to connect is that we are afraid to let go and trust in something other than the ego-self, which determines what we see of life based on the distorted beliefs we carry.

If we believe that everything we see is real—if we accept that "seeing is believing"—and what we believe is based on past lessons, then what are we really seeing? Nothing other than a limited view, and on that view we base all our assumptions, then act out accordingly. In the process of acting out, we carry guilt that we subconsciously endeavor to remove through judging, blaming, or reacting in some way. So, what do we really see, and how are we choosing to live?

If someone says or does something that you don't like, or they react badly for no apparent reason … of course you will be upset. If there were a way of observing the situation from a neutral position, rather than a set position, would you not then look at the event objectively and ask relevant questions like … do they react like this to others? Is what they said or did that harmful to yourself? Are they crying out for attention? From this neutral position, would you not see their reactions as merely their own unresolved issues (envy, jealousy, or insecurity, perhaps) expressing themselves outwardly with little or no thought as to who may be impacted?

When you have these simple tools available showing you "what to do," you don't see life through a tunnel or act out overzealously; rather, they allow you to "quiet the thought," look inward, and reason before responding. This in itself maintains a vital confidence in Self and allows life to be truly lived and enjoyed. A free mind is a mind liberated from past conditioning.

These characteristics, and the events that follow, can then be seen differently. And the great news is that you won't see what you once saw ... and you will acquire the crucial element of *choice*. It is through choice that everything changes.

The difference between an ego state (unconscious and unaware) and a connected inner state (conscious and aware) is that if we are able to connect within before we respond, to quiet the mind, the way to respond will come from within. The need to look outwardly first is replaced by a sustainable and reliable source: Self. What better guide could we have than the inner Self—inner knowledge that is capable of always delivering the desired outcome. A wholly trustworthy source we forget to listen to when the external noise of an ego-self is far too loud.

Occurrences that once could trigger challenging emotions then reactions? ... Simply no longer a problem! You are literally choosing another path that clearly reveals your power to easily dissipate any adverse circumstance! *You* choose how to respond in any particular situation—to respond with kindness, regardless of what is said or done, or simply set a boundary to let others know when something is unacceptable ... but the important note here is that your choice will be a considered, conscious response that preserves your peace of mind, and no longer a thoughtless, unconscious reaction that does not.

In a state of inner Self-trust and awareness, we are able to hold on to the truth of our reality and allow others their own realities. Life must still go on, but learning starts and ends with the inner Self.

Inner Self-connection means knowing that there is a greater purpose to all life. We learn something from every event that happens: that is why accepting before responding is the key to abundance!

If we impose limits on how we respond to the experiences within our life, a less-than-abundant outcome will result, leaving us forever wanting. Similarly, if, by trusting in our Self responses, we feel we are capable of doing something—because we become more aware of life and its purpose—we cannot help but manifest abundance; so many of life's gifts will present themselves to us: connectedness, love, peace of mind, joy, and a sustainable, dependable foundation.

Reality 1: Challenging past—EGO develops—limiting beliefs—tunnel vision—unconscious overzealous reactions—lucky-dip outcome—suffering highs and lows

Reality 2: Awareness of past—choice to change—inner Self-trust and connection—wider view of life—conscious action through awareness—abundance—sustainable peace and joy!

Our perceptions determine what we think, what we think determines what we see, what we see we dissect and evaluate, what we value determines what we want, what we want determines our actions.

If our perceptions are distorted, the value we place on what we see becomes distorted and we may then fixate on a mere perception or idea. As quickly as we value something (a mere idea) we can devalue something, and this is how we can turn perception around … with a mere willingness to do so! What is important is that we endeavor to understand our most basic thought process—our perceptions.

We must face the origins of our fears, if we are to remove fear from our lives and prevent any overzealous behaviors. A simple thing to say, more challenging to do, but with a powerful positive impact. But note—the only truly challenging aspect of it is making the decision to question and observe.

The next time you are the focus of another person's reaction … look for a new perception before responding. Perceive just for this one occasion that maybe it's not about you…? In other words, "observe without evaluating." Observe as if this were a stage performance … you might sooner or later find yourself laughing at the situation that you once deemed a personal attack or deeply serious. The outcome in some (not all) cases may be that the other person's reaction quickly dissipates and they offer an apology.

If you find this exercise challenging because you simply can't seem to stop your immediate responses, then I ask you to try this

… hold back on responding for just a few moments while you *quiet the mind!*

It is through taking the time to truly observe the reality around us that we are able to start perceiving differently. Once we perceive differently, we think differently … so practice is the key, and every response you need to make—of which there may be many in any one day—is an opportunity to practice.

In observing our thoughts and behaviors, and the behaviors of others, we will soon ascertain which responses bring us peace and which responses bring unease. In observing others, we learn about our own behaviors. Once again, our behaviors will lead back to our thoughts, which we can then reassess.

A Key Driver in Life

Our purpose in life is to find a sustainable peace and joy in our life. It is our sole purpose—why or how could it be any other way? If you had peace and joy in your life, what else would you need? So, don't we owe it to ourselves to really look at our thought processes, endeavor to perceive clearly through awareness, change our behaviors and our thoughts when we feel troubled, and work on undoing the many layers of misconceptions our past holds us prisoner to?

Imagine now, if you will, the following scenario:

You feel prepared and confident to approach life differently, confident in Self, fearless in communicating regardless of life's challenges—unfazed—an observer. You know that the path to your peace of mind is upholding this new reality in order to maintain life's greatest gift—peace of mind.

As you arrive at work, or when you get home, you greet people in an open, happy way—you offer a simple smile or welcoming eyes to greet them. You know that any challenge is part and parcel of life, and each of us is doing our best with the understanding we have at the time. Your efforts for the most part will be well received (not always, just as we might occasionally misperceive someone else's bad day as a slingshot at us—as we used to do all the time).

Because you are more aligned, your thoughts aren't consumed by tunnel vision, wasting endless time obsessing on fixing something you perceive to be troubling you, something outside you, in the hope of fixing the difficult feelings you are experiencing within, trying to fill a cup that was already full. As a result, others respond to you generously, you feel connected, you possess more energy and motivation—your mental energy is freed up for abstract thinking and creativity. A zest for life develops.

That's the scenario of Self-connection, the formula to living life to the full.

When we change our perception through our willingness and practice, and we witness the monumental changes that then occur, our motivation to truly live life becomes a key driver to continue.

Does our life not then become a process of living in the present, consciously manifesting the best life has to offer, rather than continually reacting to the negative feelings triggered by something someone said that we didn't like or by someone not doing something we expected? How much time do we waste because we're attending to our self-created perceptions and thoughts about past events, or what someone said or did? How much of life do we miss out on because we're consumed by trying to guess what another person is thinking or doing?

Aren't we then free to do more of what we really want to do with our days, such as pursuing our passions or hobbies, observing life, connecting authentically with others and enjoying the benefits they bring? To spend quality time with people we care about, or just simply take a little time for Self?

Won't you feel more grateful for such a life, and for who's in it, and for what you have, if you stop for just a moment and quiet the mind when you feel things are off-kilter, in order to respond with inner confidence, rather than reacting?

The question is: how much of our time and mental energy do we allow to be consumed by distorted beliefs about how life "must be" instead of accepting life and allowing it to unfold organically?

When disconnected from the inner Self, we have a tendency to think obsessively, to do certain things repeatedly, and to get caught up in frequent conflicts and human dramas in order to validate our distorted reasons for continuing to think, say, and do the same things we have always said, thought, and done without feeling better for the effort.

Why don't we ask *why*? Why do I feel unfulfilled? Why am I constantly anxious, tired, or frustrated by life? Because it would reveal the lie we are living in. But don't we want to discover that it has been our own choices that have kept us in this mindset?

Choose now to see things through new eyes, particularly becoming more consciously aware of who and what you have—spending more time with those you love and value, seeing kindness in others, showing compassion for how others express themselves without taking it personally, being grateful for what you have. Also, take a moment in your day to smell the roses and spend a little time with your Self in silent prayer or meditation, or perhaps just in doing things that please you.

EXERCISE
A Time to Reflect and Create Balance

Sit quietly, close your eyes, and breathe deeply. For a few moments, allow yourself to rest your mind by going within to experience the silence of the inner Self.

Continue to breathe for several moments without forcing your breath into any particular pattern of inhalation and exhalation, until your breath becomes quieter.

Then open your eyes and ask any of the following questions:

- How much time do I spend cultivating love with those close to me?

- How much time do I spend letting go and truly observing?

- How often do I relax into a meaningful dialogue without feeling the need to exude great energy, opinions, and judgment?

- Can I relax and accept what happens without reacting?

- Am I able to listen and love for longer than a short moment in time?

- Do I feel grateful for those around me, especially those closest to me?

- Can I give a compliment easily—and do I? Do I look for the best in people?

- Do I appreciate my life, and what I have around me, and feel grateful for it?

- Do I express gratitude, and if so how often?

- Do I take a little "me-time"—observing nature, stopping for a moment to enjoy life around me?

- Do I have faith in a reality beyond the physical? Do I know or feel that I am supported by the universe?

- Can I find peace in my life or know how to acquire it?

To end a pattern of conflicted thoughts and behaviors, we must begin by observing the conflicted mind. As we do so repeatedly, we gradually learn to notice the behaviors that are preventing us from living our lives to the fullest.

Sit quietly, reflect for a few moments, and then end the session.

Ending Conflict

The mind is the property of our inner Self. When we are separated from the inner Self, we instinctively feel fear. We begin to seek alternatives to finding support and meaning in life. Hence, the ego exists—not in a unified mind, but in one separated from reality—a mind separated from its true source.

Separated from its true source, the mind feels rejected by something; it doesn't know what. Because we feel alone and unsupported in the world, we fear life—feel we are subject to the whim of life and not the creator of our life.

No one is strong enough to get through life successfully, happily, with a highly conflicted mind, feeling alone, and constantly feeling the need to fight to survive and be happy!

EXERCISE
Ending Conflict

When we are ready to end a conflict, we begin by opening the door to an authentic connection with Self and others—we unify our minds. Feel the effects. Try the following three actions:

1. Observe your reality without evaluating it. Just for one day, regardless of what is said or what you see, hold on to your own sense of reality and know that you are being supported.

2. Accept life in whatever way it is presented to you. Just allow whatever happens to you and around you to be as it is. As best you can, drop all negative thoughts, which represent your resistance to life as it is. Any unease you feel is resistance. Make a conscious effort to let go and live for just this one day.

3. Offer love and kindness at every turn. When you think you are right and someone else's view differs in the extreme, if this opinion is unshakeable, practice being "kind" instead of needing to be "right." Understand that you can accept someone else's viewpoint as valid to them without taking it "on board" yourself.

When we offer love to others, we accept them for who they are. We are observing without evaluating, embracing our own truth, and, importantly, choosing to be kind over being right. We don't have to assert our viewpoint over someone else's in most situations. Most views are not a matter of life or death!

As we learn to accept life and to understand that other people's views, regardless of how they're expressed, are something outside of us that we do not necessarily need to

---

take personally, ultimately we acquire a wonderful sense of peace and love—because what we give out will always return in kind.

EXERCISE
A Simple Practice for Letting Go and Surrendering

Here is an exercise to practice each day, for a few moments, that has the power to significantly change your day for the better. It's an exercise that will heighten your sense of trust in Self and thereafter your trust in a universal, supportive, spiritual energy that has the power to create miracles.

When you wake up, ask that your day be blessed. Then sit quietly, beginning to breathe and relax the body, and follow all the steps below. You may have the urge to get out of the chair and start a day full of (overzealous) activities from the get-go—stop yourself.

In order to free yourself of anxiety and concern, you need to institute practices that reverse old thinking—this is what we are attempting to do here. Practicing this will exponentially create the changes you desire, in a fraction of the time they would otherwise take. So don't give in to your urges; rather, create new habits through the consistent practice of a simple technique.

First, sit quietly, and think about the many things you are grateful for—who is around you, what you have achieved, what successes you have had in work or play, the relationships you've acquired, the challenges that you've recently overcome. Gratitude focuses the mind away from tunnel vision and the need to be overzealous, dispensing with the time-wasting that accompanies these misgivings and going straight to the end desire—manifesting more of what you are grateful for.

Second, sit in silence, for five minutes or so; close your

Exercise continues on next page

Exercise continued

eyes and breathe deeply into your diaphragm. As your body relaxes, let your breathing become shallower and follow the breath with your thoughts. As the breath becomes quieter and shallower, allow your thoughts to subside. The body will relax. Just trust and let go.

Third, let new thoughts follow this moment in silence, to prepare your day and enable the creative thinking that will manifest the best outcome for you. Think about how you wish your day to be—for example:

Let my day flow smoothly, my work go without drama, and my relationships be easy and loving. Let me recognize those in my life I most value. Let me not react today. Instead, allow me to observe without evaluating. Look after those I love so I need not worry. Help me let go of negative thoughts as I recognize them, help me learn to accept all that happens and know there is a greater reason for it, help me to live without fear today, and help me express love to others today. May my day start and end peacefully.

Effectively, what you are seeking to do is end each session by making clear three desires, to make your day wonderful:

1. **How do you wish to feel?** (peaceful, joyful, happy, confident, hopeful)

2. **What would you ideally like to happen in your day?** (success?—what part would you like to be successful—verbalize it! E.g. health of your children, resolution of a challenging relationship)

3. **What do you wish to experience?** (inner strength to change your perceptions, more love, no judgments)

   How do you wish to be supported today? The choice is yours—so ask for it. There are no rules. Do not let overzealous behavior spoil your day and consume your time—make clear choices that will allow you to be in control of your day, and your life.

Release your thoughts, breathe, and end with a prayer if that is what you are used to, or end with a moment or two in silence. When you decide you are ready, open your eyes and go about your day!

At night, reflect on all the things about your day that went well—and if they didn't, reflect on why not. Could you have managed anything differently? Most certainly, the exercises in this book will impact your life in miraculous ways—so take the time to reflect and notice. Witnessing the beneficial impact of these exercises will give you the strength to continue.

Keep practicing each day, morning and night! Be alert to positive changes occurring around you … seeing is believing, after all … then be grateful for them!

Just stay with it! What you are doing is consciously manifesting more of the same!

EXERCISE
Compassion: A Simple Exercise to Find Peace When You Feel Wronged

The purpose of this exercise is to find compassion for anyone you feel you have little or no compassion for.

Just sit quietly and concentrate on creating a positive affirmation or finding a positive attribute about that person. Once you've done so, allow yourself to feel whatever you feel.

Please try this simple exercise now. Be authentic. After you send out your loving message or experience appreciation for the person, do not return to criticism. Endeavor to drop your resentments and judgments.

Exercise continues on next page

Exercise continued

Remember that this is about you finding peace within your own mind and heart. So it is most important to remember what you feel in the moment after you experience a peaceful or loving thought. You are creating peacefulness through the choice you made!

Whenever I feel resentment toward someone I feel has wronged me, this is my favorite way to deal with my feelings. I simply sit quietly, go within, and relax my mind. Then I send a very positive affirmation and loving response to the individual. Reminding myself that the purpose is to find peace, and knowing it is an opportunity to learn how to release myself from fear, I bring the perceived cause of my unease to mind and say, "I love you, [Name], and accept you as you are."

In your own practice, when a fear-based thought has been replaced with a love-based thought about someone, hold on to your grace by going quietly about your day. If the negative thought comes to mind again during the day, just drop it as soon as you notice it. Dropping a thought may seem hard at first—but rest assured, it does get easier!

This practice strengthens the peacefulness you experience from releasing your unease. If you practice frequently, you will soon begin to recognize that your thoughts determine your reality and your opportunities for peace.

It's a simple practice that's highly effective!

Faith is love: love of self, love of others, love of life, love of a higher power/God/a universal energy, and love of the power it holds for us. It is time to free ourselves of our limiting beliefs about what we can be, and to start to rebuild our faith—not only in ourselves, but in all life and each other. This is the greater meaning to life that helps us accept life and each other. *The more love we give, the more supported we feel, the more meaning we give life, and the more joy we experience.*

Let's observe the behaviors that lead us to our fear-based thoughts—the ones that cause us to react to life and others in ways that keep us from our full potential—and transform them.

Let's learn about the love and inner power we possess when we connect within. As we have discussed, when we observe the many limiting beliefs that cause us to behave in the ways we do—ways that create more separation and the unease and discontent that follows it—we can find the intention to change. We can, through new ego-awareness and self-observation, teach our minds to reconnect to the true Self. It is the true Self in us that expresses love.

Let's observe the thoughts behind the feelings and behaviors that affect our lives and our level of faith. Let us remember that it is our faith that will allow us to live passionately and lovingly within life.

Shed the ego, question its fears, observe its behaviors, and you will begin to shatter the myths and beliefs you have held on to out of fear. Let the ego go and live passionately in this moment.

> *"No force except your own will is strong enough*
> *or worthy enough to guide you. In this you are as*
> *free as God, and must remain so forever."*
> *A Course in Miracles*

CHAPTER FIVE

VICTIM STATE

"Often, the best gifts we would ever receive in
life are wrapped in the worst packages."
Khayri R.R. Woulfe

Every action we take in life, we ultimately take for a greater purpose: to evolve and find our own path to Self-love, establish inner connection, and put an end to the fear-based reality we have come to believe is so real.

If we do not understand the ego-self, or the way our life plays out, with all our ups and downs, how can we be expected to understand others, be free in the present, and live life peacefully, gracefully, and abundantly?

I have enjoyed reading the work of psychologist Stephen Karpman, in which he writes about the *Karpman drama triangle.* Through this model of relationship, he shows the impact that a negative mindset has on us and on those we interact with—especially in our primary relationships. A negative mindset affects the tone of our interactions and explains why, how, and to whom we are attracted. In reflecting on my own life and relationships, as well as on the lives of people I have observed, I find it simplest to reference his ideas through my own understanding of the impact of the victim state, which is the subject of this chapter.

The Karpman triangle shows how we interact with others based on the mental scripts we have formed about who we are, what we believe the world is like, how we relate to the world, and how we are treated. Research suggests that each of us has formed our mental scripts by the time we are four or five years of age. A script is formed in response to what we are told, what we experience, and how we interpret our experiences from our own internal frame of reference.

Our psychological scripts support us in unconsciously playing games that become the drivers behind our behavioral interactions.

Bear in mind that not all scripts are negative. However, our negative scripts support our limiting beliefs about ourselves and other people in the world around us.

The Karpman drama triangle is a wonderful way of looking at the drama and conflict that play out in the world from our ego state of unconsciousness. There are three positions in the drama triangle: **victim**, **rescuer**, and **persecutor**. Each role has a set of characteristics that support it, as follows:

The victim or martyr: This role is characterized by feelings of helplessness, hopelessness, and powerlessness. In this state, we feel we cannot take care of ourselves, so we put our fate in the hands of those we believe are more powerful than we are. Victims do not think clearly or try to solve problems, believing that their neediness and strong negative emotions prevent them from doing so. Often, victims' early childhood experiences have left them feeling victimized and unable to solve their own problems. As they become disconnected from their source of knowing, they also lose inner Self-love and trust.

The rescuer or hero/caretaker: This role is characterized by feelings of sentimentality; a belief that others' needs are more important than our own; a fear of being persecuted if we don't help; a perception that others are inadequate and therefore need our help; and a strong sense that something terrible will happen if we do not help. This fear-based state originates in rescuers' childhood experiences and prevents them from ascertaining their true intentions and feelings or asking for the appropriate help they need. Their unconscious behaviors drive them to attempt to control their reality and to try very hard to make those around them feel safe and good about themselves.

The persecutor or critic: This role is characterized by anger and resentment. Persecutors think, "I'm okay, but you're not okay," "This is your fault," and "I need to take care of myself." Others suffer from being around them, as persecutors feel they need to "teach" others about their faults. Relationships suffer greatly over the long term as persecutors' punishing and judging behaviors cause others pain. Demonstrating shame-based behavior patterns, which formed early in life, persecutors are more critical of themselves than anyone else, although they fail to share this information with others. Through persecuting people, they believe, they'll be okay in "this moment." They struggle with non-acceptance of life and others, and suffer from a need to exercise power due to their lack of self-worth. They punish others because they feel unappreciated and out of control.

All three of these archetypal patterns are fear based and were formed early in life for the purpose of controlling, manipulating, and wielding power. Set these dynamics against the backdrop of powerlessness many of us typically feel, and you can see how they are responsible for creating all the drama and conflict in our lives.

From attending therapy, I eventually came to realize that it is easy to fluctuate between all three of these roles when we are living within a fear-based mentality. Think about your own behavior and beliefs—how often do you feel unappreciated, become angry, and act in ways that are negative for you and for others? Yes, we may feel okay for a short moment in time, but guilt often has the last say. Feeling the guilt caused by our behavior stimulates in us a need to rescue another person—though often not the one we feel guilty for having passively or aggressively attacked. And we may feel a need to play victim outside the relationship where the conflict occurred so as to feel validated or accepted.

It doesn't matter if a relationship is romantic, parental, or collegial, the dynamic is the same. Any expectation of validation that is not met will before long leave us feeling unappreciated, disappointed, and victimized.

In hindsight, I realize that over the course of my life I have played all three roles at different times in my different relationships—victim, rescuer, and persecutor. It's evident to me that relationships of almost any type can be based on this same model to varying degrees. The drama triangle is a very common style of interrelating.

Early twentieth-century British journalist and publisher Holbrook Jackson said, "Happiness is a form of courage," and you will need courage for the process of making intentional changes. Here, together, we will face the truth of our individual realities and set about undoing the childhood beliefs that we have perpetuated in our lives so profoundly. Everyone's belief system is unique. But the process of how we form beliefs is the same for all people: past learning. Through awareness and vigilance, as an expression of Self-love, and with understanding, we can undo our unhealthy beliefs and move on from them.

There are victims of severe abuse and harm in the world, and my heart goes out to them. Tragic circumstances, misfortune, and pain can and regularly do leave people profoundly traumatized. How do these people reconnect and find meaning in their lives? Some are successful and some are unsuccessful. People do their best to adapt. The human spirit of resilience never ceases to amaze me. Some very courageous souls have undergone enormous tragedy and become stronger and more compassionate as a result. This book is not directed at these experiences so much as at healing the emotional pain and unhealthy behavioral patterns that are among the less extreme aspects of our daily lives and relationships.

Is there a right and a wrong way to behave toward ourselves or others? That's an interesting question. A better question might be: "When are we ready to stop having the types of experiences that prevent us from living our lives and loving to the fullest?"

Before we can stop hurting ourselves and others emotionally, we must first recognize the physical experiences and behavioral patterns that clearly show where we are making choices that do not enhance our own lives or the lives of those around us. Once we notice the signs, we must find the courage to change those behaviors and embrace peacefulness and love instead.

The *victim state* is the role that can ultimately help us recognize our misgivings and the limitations we have placed on our lives and relationships. This chapter is about observing behaviors in which we are being or playing the victim.

Many of us have suffered trauma in our lives. Trauma is a subjective response to painful events that can create desperate feelings that make us perceive ourselves as victims. Left unrecognized, the mentality of a victim state causes us to feel pain and anxiety, express the fears we hold on to after the traumatic events are over, and attempt to manipulate the environment around us to get our inner needs met—although we do not necessarily recognize what our true needs are. One of the biggest needs of a person who has been traumatized is the *need for safety.*

Self-identified victims constantly seek out others who they believe can save them from the fear they hold within. Expressing their need to feel fulfilled, they use control tactics, manipulation, self-pity, and anger. This is the lesson we learned earlier in life of how to get our unmet needs heard. In the past, making others feel bad may have gotten us something we wanted, such as gaining a level of acceptance, being noticed, or feeling important or more loved. The drama of making others feel bad when we're unhappy gives us a sense of aliveness that feels better to us than the frustrations we normally feel in our lives. Part of the role of being a victim is blaming others if our needs are not met or for how our lives have worked out (or how we believe they are working out). This is a communication pattern we have become used to.

We can begin to perceive ourselves as victims early in life or late in life. Children who grow up having everything done for them and being overindulged would not necessarily feel victimized by this experience. But they might later on in their lives, as they attempt to function on their own outside their original environment, when the support they are used to is no longer there.

A young man I met many years ago had everything done for him as a child. His mother's desire to do things for him was more important to her than her son's needs. At age twenty-two, he reported feeling incapable of doing anything for himself. He said he couldn't adequately function in everyday society. He felt like a victim and couldn't live comfortably within his own skin.

Finding someone who will take on the role of rescuing us from the pains of life can mean we create a relationship where we become a victim again.

Just prior to my divorce, during turbulent periods of my relationship with my ex-wife, I slowly began to recognize the signs of my behaviors and the effects of those behaviors, not only on her but also on me. They certainly robbed me of my peace of mind. Fully recognizing those behaviors was vital to my well-being and the relationship. However, because I was busy playing out the role of fixer, or demanding things from my wife, I couldn't see or hear what she was trying to say to me. I would label her a victim, though actually, pre-divorce, I was the one playing the role of the victim, constantly trying to meet her needs based on my expectations of what those were, as opposed to what she was actually telling me she needed. Playing the victim, I unknowingly built up resentment about not feeling loved or appreciated for my efforts. I couldn't see that she was expressing the same need to feel loved and appreciated.

In hindsight, feeling like a victim myself, I readily communicated my hurts to my wife through anger. I held on to my resentment and blamed my wife for causing the breakdown. In short, I couldn't and wouldn't take responsibility. The constant push-pull dynamic between us, often at the most subliminal levels of our interactions, was draining and also blocked any desire for peace or to revive a sense of healing and love. Finally, though, I needed answers more than anything—answers that I found when I looked deep within, recognized my behaviors, and measured them against my true desires. I identified what was important to me, and I made a conscious decision from the perspective of that inner position, that inner Self-knowing—to look at her needs in relation to my own and understand them equally. Given time and my willingness to commit to change, the relationship would take on a whole new meaning.

There was a period after my marriage ended when I felt utterly hopeless and incapable. That was when I woke up to the fact that, as I have shared with many people over the years, I had played the victim to my circumstances, feeling throughout my life as if I didn't have choices and not knowing what to do other than become angry and frustrated, criticizing and blaming the people around me for how things were working out. Looking back over my life, I identified the victim mentality that had in turn often compelled me to try to rescue others: I was driven by the belief that I knew the way to lead a successful life and thought I could help. In the process, I often attracted people willing to discover a different reality than the one they were frustrated by, but my rescuing efforts and expectations led me to end up feeling like a victim myself. For example, helping people succeed in business was a gift of mine—a gift that I have since come to realize was born out of necessity to escape my painful past. While it was not all bad, of course, ultimately the personal pressure of sharing so much time left me without any energy to give where it would be truly appreciated. The motivation to succeed, in order to escape the past, and the overzealous behavior all took their toll and the truth eventually sprang to the surface—as it always does.

Emotional pain projected outward causes us to lose our life balance. For this reason, we must face it head on. Many people have felt and displayed the characteristics of the victim mentality—to different degrees, of course—at different periods in their lives. Learning to recognize these behaviors is a vital step toward healing our minds and overriding this debilitating and limiting mindset when it is activated.

The Life of a Victim: Becoming Aware

If we are in the victim state, we have the capacity to manipulate others to rescue us from a fate we feel we have no control over. Haven't we all felt this way at times—as if we are the victim? Felt helpless in love or life? Felt an intense need to be validated or loved because we don't feel it within? When we are in the victim state, our demand for love can be consuming.

In fact, when we play the victim we have disconnected from our inner Self—we fear the unknown and have no sustainable foundation. We too easily judge, criticize, or blame others, believing we are disadvantaged in life. Often, others become the target of our attacks for a myriad of reasons: wanting validation or acceptance, wanting to feel loved, or simply needing a sympathetic ear to vent to. We become lost in negative thoughts and wrapped up in behavioral patterns that only serve to fuel the fear, anxiety, and neediness we are feeling.

There is no cure for an unhealed mind other than the recognition of its own pattern. For a person caught in the pattern of the victim state, those signs are hard to notice at first. A victim is blind to the truth. As victims, we keep up the facade and choose to ignore the truth, blaming others and punishing them for their part in our perceived misfortune.

Of course, this doesn't work well. If you have ever tried to help a person who feels like a victim, you know how utterly frustrating it can be, because they can always find more reasons to sink back into the role. The rescuers (as they are referred to in the drama triangle) become the victims' perfect partners.

The good news is that nothing will get you closer to the truth of your own reality than this victim–rescuer relationship, which is highly demanding and exhausting for all involved!

As victims, we cannot be helped by others; we must start the process of developing understanding ourselves. Blaming, attacking, or manipulating our rescuer partners does not help us understand our victim state; it just enables us to continue it.

As victims, we leave others confused and frustrated by our actions. We seem to be able to keep up the facade, intellectualize our reasons for doing detrimental things, find others who will justify our actions, and—at the moment of our choosing—play the hand of self-pity.

We must recognize the effects that our childhoods or other experiences have had on our lives, understand why we feel victimized, if we are to change course and find the peace and joy we desperately search for. How we were treated as children becomes disguised from the world by the strategies we cleverly concocted and then practiced over and over, often without knowing what we were doing. Because of our difficult experiences, we disconnected from the inner Self and felt alone or afraid. Growing up became a struggle. Since then, we have carried unease, anxiety, and fears within us, blocking ourselves from any Self-healing or understanding—blocking our ego-selves from the *instinctively* knowing *Self* and subsequently the world around us. In the absence of inner Self-connection and trust, we don't know how to act appropriately to genuinely enhance our well-being and the authenticity of our relationships.

Here is the really good news: at any moment we choose, we can make the decision to observe and question how we are feeling and behaving, and take almost immediately the first step required to feel *peace of mind*. When we experience positive new feelings, like peace of mind, joy, and calmness, we plant the seed of change that will ultimately and unquestionably grow!

The first step, that of choosing, is the hardest, of course. We must recognize the pain or unease we are experiencing and take proper mental note—observe it—and remember iti when we feel it. Then we must be willing to experience a different reality instead—when willingness is maintained, we start to ask relevant questions.

It is difficult for us to make this choice while we are caught up in the past, feeling victimized by our circumstances and unwilling to accept that we are responsible for our lives and behaviors.

Like all archetypal behaviors, victim behaviors are hard to switch off when we have become dependent on them to *feel*. They seem to hold in place the only reality we know. Dare we question it? What would we be left with otherwise?

We play the victim unknowingly, always maintaining a sense of control against the backdrop of the fears we live with. There is no escape from this fear until we acknowledge the truth of why we feel incapable of dealing with our lives, and why it is so hard for us to face the truth of the past. Why would victims wish to remember their pain and feelings of helplessness? They have their lives sorted out now, they have a level of control—or so they think—and they do not want to let go of that control—it is a perceived lifeline away from a difficult past. Denial is easier than facing the truth of distorted reasoning.

To understand the victim-state mentality, we only need to look at the reality of our lives. Look at the unease we live with as a consequence of the reality we see, a reality based on misguided thoughts. Stop believing that this unease is normal. It isn't—in fact, it's messing everything up! Look at the numerous physical signs—these can easily be observed, and they show us clearly that our perceptions have to change considerably before our desires can be met—before peace, love, and joy can become the foundation of our lives.

What must change? Here is a list of victim behaviors we can observe and immediately change if we decide to face the truth of our reality and improve our lives. These are the behaviors we must alter if we want love, joy, and peace of mind to replace the fear and anxiety we customarily express:

- Don't like what we hear so we say nothing

- Agree with others so they will like us

- Pity ourselves and express it often

- Feel we need to discuss our personal lives with others to get them to accept our behaviors

- Constantly feel anxious

- Constantly criticize and blame others; in other words, try to exert power over them to compensate for the powerlessness we feel

- Manipulate others into taking responsibility for our happiness

- Put constant and undue expectations on others

- Communicate in ways that make others react negatively— for example, in anger—in order to justify our own behaviors

- Value other people's opinions more than our own— constantly looking for approval, needing to be accepted

- Judge everything others do

- Try to be perfect

- Perceive ourselves as unlovable—constantly feel the need to be loved

People with a victim mindset are clever at finding other people's emotional triggers. A battle of wills, as misguided as such battles always are, often consumes a relationship, leading the people involved to trigger and retrigger one another. The relationship is lost to fears that belong to the past, as each person endeavors to secure the moral high ground. In the long term, such a relationship can only implode, which is why it is so important to recognize the fear, be willing to change, and become aware of the behaviors that create these toxic, highly triggering situations.

We need to recognize when we are in *victim state*. It can occur at any time, and when it does, negative thoughts seem to escalate. In the victim state, we are likely to make things up without knowing the facts. If we are to consciously create significant and pleasurable change in our lives, we must observe the behaviors that lead to our victimized patterns of thought. We can change by making a clear decision to observe, assess, and reframe those thoughts.

Change starts with Self-love and expands from there. Our thoughts then maintain this love by leading us to act responsibly. No matter how it is perceived at first, this love will always create a positive outcome. An outcome that will be observable and rewarding.

The Victim, the Rescuer, and Their Relationship

In the game of rescuing a victim, there can be no winners! Not until those involved become aware.

The relationship between victims and rescuers was so well explained to me while I was sitting in a barber's chair one rainy Tuesday morning, listening to my barber, Peter, tell me about certain friends of his—friends who weren't respecting his space or his time with his young family.

He was frustrated because they would not respect his boundaries. Instead, when these friends were with him they would do what they had always done together in the past— take drugs, drink alcohol, be noisy in his home, and make excessive demands on his time.

For some time he had noticed that each time he left the company of these friends he would feel somewhat depressed. His energy was depleted by being around them, until he no longer had any energy left for his family. His communication with his family deteriorated as a consequence, and his family life really started to be affected. Ultimately, he noticed a change in his relationship with his spouse each time he'd spent time with them.

He went on to explain to me, "I have a cup filled with love, and what I found was that these friends demanded more than a fair share, as if nothing was ever enough, needing more and more of my attention." Literally, he said, he gave and gave, and slowly the relationships drained the cup, leaving little for those that meant and deserved so much more.

Finally, some fifteen months on from his first observation of his friends' behaviors and the effect they were having on him and his wife, Peter decided that enough was enough. As he said to me, "I only had one cup of love to give and I decided to give that cup to the ones I love most."

So he spoke to these friends about their behavior. But he found that the friends of old did not listen to him express his need for a change—he saw no change in them, and their conversation began to sound as if he were playing an old video.

He had explained to them what was important to him. He had told them that he would give his time to them, but only if they respected the boundaries of the friendship and the changes that had occurred in his life. In his words, if they replenished his cup by respecting his changed life—a loving act—he would maintain the friendships.

It eventually became clear that he would need to disassociate from these friends. In the end, for his own well-being and that of his wife, he simply stopped seeing them. His reasoning was that to allow others to impose their will on him, especially if it impacted his relationship with his wife, was no longer an option. To have ignored their behavior or allowed the victim mentality to manipulate his reasoning would have been to fail to value what was truly valuable! Self-love, love of what is important to us, is not selfishness. Rather, it is an act of love that creates harmony in the world around us.

His friends were angry; one in particular, someone he had known for twenty years, was very offended by his decision. But Peter stuck to his decision.

After he'd limited those friendships, Peter decided to surround himself with new friends who could fill his cup— through common interests shared with his family. Never again, he vowed, would he allow those who just took from him to keep taking, even if it meant not seeing them again. No longer would he allow himself to feel victimized by another person imposing their will on him; nor would he allow others to play the victim with him—especially if their expectations cost him what he truly valued and loved.

This is what we need to take notice of in the life story above: we must follow Peter's lead in surrounding ourselves with people who replenish our cups ... fill them with love, and make a conscious decision to do so, to ensure we make the same commitment to ourselves.

EXERCISE
A Quick Self-Assessment

Stop for a moment and observe your reality.

Sit quietly, go within, and rest your mind. Change begins with the courage to look within and be honest about how you view your relationships and assess what is really important to you. As you do so, ask, "Do my behaviors display victim-like patterns?"

You will recognize a victim state by the unease you feel from simply asking this question.

If you catch yourself making excuses or blaming others without trying to understand their point of view, then you will be caught in a cycle of negativity and consider yourself to be a victim.

As we have already discussed, there may be perfectly sound reasons to feel like a victim—people do suffer real trauma in life. However, in this exercise we focus on those times when we *feel* like victims but really we are just trying not to face our reality ... that is, the truth behind our unease that causes us to project our pain outward, blame others, and feel victimhood. This is what we need to recognize. It is in this recognition that our behaviors change, and then so too our reality.

If the answer to the question above is yes, you may be stopping yourself from creating authentic, loving relationships that will enhance the quality of your life.

Resolving the Internalized Pain We Feel

Unless we face the past courageously and understand *why* we think, say, and do the things we think, say, and do, we can never understand *how* we can change.

It is through our inner connection that we come to know what feels right and what feels wrong for us; and this is how we learn to establish healthy boundaries to protect ourselves from the many variables that life throws at us. Healthy boundaries enable us to express love outwardly, and they help us reserve the energy we need to live with zest and share love with the people who are important to us.

Healthy Boundaries Change Perception

Think about a time when you felt you were a victim. What did you need? Did you find yourself constantly feeling anxious, worried, and withdrawn? Did you have a sense of wanting to give up?

We must establish positive mental boundaries for ourselves in order to maintain our desire for change. Without clear and positive emotional and physical boundaries, change is more difficult. Change is behavioral.

Disengage from negative thoughts. Establish a healthy boundary. Protect what needs protecting: your peace of mind and your willingness to receive and express love, especially with those most important to you—they give you your sense of balance and deserve your love and care!

In this way, we become more aware that the adapted ego-self we created, to protect us from our many misperceptions, is getting in the way of our path to peace and true abundance. Fortunately, love is inherently who we are. Thus, we already know love better than we think we do. When we begin to express love rather than fear, we will feel (and then see) the difference it creates in our lives.

Having knowledge of what we want helps us to set healthy boundaries. Setting boundaries means that we don't let the fear-based thoughts and behaviors of self and others get between us and the people who are important to us. It is through our awareness and willingness to set boundaries that we take back control of our reality and, importantly, stop enabling or disengage from others, who must then question their own reality—this is a gift you give in the true sense.

There is not one action we take that is not driven by the motivation to be loved and accepted!

Because we attract relationships that give us the opportunity to fulfill our inner needs—often as a means to fix events in our past—those relationships will bring us more of the painful experiences that echo that past, and the past will naturally keep repeating itself. If we do not face our own victim-state mentality and express Self-control, love, kindness, and understanding in place of drama, conflict, and manipulation, our relationships will deteriorate, our anxiety or unease will continue, and we will miss out on the abundance and sense of self-worth and confidence we each desire.

When learning to set healthy boundaries, we must remember that as victims we become masterful at deception, including self-deception, because the ego that we have created is itself masterful at it, often masking our true feelings (hopelessness, neediness, unease, and pain) with behaviors that cast blame and guilt onto others. In other words, we do not take responsibility for our feelings or behaviors. So, when someone sets a boundary for us or we set a boundary for our own behaviors it can be very hard to comply with.

Any uneasy feeling can alert us to the need to change a behavior within a relationship—and this can make all the difference. It does not matter where you are in a relationship right now: change can occur, and the relationship can often be salvaged, if it is seen in a different light of consciousness.

We must stop the fear by recognizing the truth behind the patterns of conflict and drama within our relationships. It is when we know that fear is something we have learned that we apply reason and change for the better. This enables us to stop reacting thoughtlessly and instead change the behavior.

Setting Healthy Boundaries for Your Own Behaviors When You Feel Like a Victim

Here are a few behaviors we can avoid or stop as soon as we catch ourselves doing them:

- Self-loathing, self-criticism, and self-pity

- Accepting put-downs from others

- Blaming others as a means to get something, anything

- Getting caught up in a cycle of negativity, obsessive thoughts, replaying the day's events over and over

- Listening to or expressing drama

- Letting our thoughts run away with us when it feels as if we aren't getting what we want, creating a greater degree of anxiety

- Expecting others to meet our expectations and becoming angry and frustrated when they do not

- Reacting without adequately discussing what's going on

- Refusing to listen to others express their points of view

- Experiencing excessive highs and lows

- Constantly defending our actions

- Constantly seeking validation for our actions and ideas

Our personal victim-state behaviors need to be replaced with responsible, loving behaviors. Patience will be required as we undo our past beliefs and give our relationships a chance of healthy recovery. This patience will largely be directed toward inner Self-awareness and ego-self learning, as well as toward finding the courage to change some of our age-old beliefs around how life needs to be lived.

Remember, life is in balance when you feel a consistent level of joy and peace within. If you don't, then there are things you must work on. Something is not right.

Setting boundaries is an important aspect of forming and sustaining any new beliefs. Boundaries are needed to stop you from repeatedly acting out past behaviors, giving you time to embrace change and witness the difference this change makes to your life and those you love.

If positive change occurs in *you*, the natural consequence is that over time it must also occur in others—regardless of any immediate pushback or anyone's refusal to accept your change at first.

Communicate with love and forgiveness, not blame and resentment. Accept others, but don't accept behaviors from yourself or others that limit your desire to engage in authentically loving communication.

You don't need to take the "moral high ground"; what you need is to own your own ground and to hold that ground lovingly.

Express no resentment or anger toward others. When communicating with someone, use words that reflect your own needs, not your feelings about the other person. For example, when expressing a verbal boundary, to begin with say:

- "I'm not feeling okay, and this is what I need from you to help me feel okay about me."

- "I don't blame you. I take responsibility for how I feel. I would like to communicate with you."

- "Please allow me the space I need to sit with my feelings."

Also, don't be afraid to ask the other person to take responsibility for what they say and do as well. We all slip up and we all fall back into patterns of expressing blame and anger. Recognize when you are doing this, and simply stop doing it. When things are poorly received, give yourself plenty of love instead and try again later.

This is when we must keep our courage up and stay with the truth, the truth that we are no longer willing to be unhappy, blaming, anxious, fearful, restricted, worthless, hurt, or limited in a relationship.

Make the decision to accept yourself, with all your imperfections, and let go of any guilt you may feel. The past is gone—recognize it, learn to forgive it, and believe that life starts afresh for you right now. If you fail, and regress to feeling guilt and unease and act out poorly, catch yourself, set a boundary, and then commit to starting the process of change again. Regression to old patterns of behaviors, thoughts, and feelings is a vital and integral part of healing. Trial and error are part of the process of undoing past beliefs and replacing them with new ones.

Go slowly! Be kind to the ego-self, nurture Self-love, and you will find the courage to let go. Feel what feels right versus what feels wrong as you regress—then sit with it for a time, observing the effects on you and the impact it may have on others—observe how they are feeling.

Find that inner Self-connection. It is by falling down and getting back up again and again that your path to success and Self-fulfillment will become guaranteed.

Stop unhealthy behaviors. Set healthy boundaries and hold your own ground. Choose to no longer live in fear: fear of abandonment, never having enough, and worthlessness. Choose to change—choose positive thoughts—have no fear, embrace it. To live fearlessly is to live with complete love of Self, and in that, love for others—be kind to your ego-self as well as others.

EXERCISE
A Moment of Restfulness

It will take enormous courage to face the past. But that is what you need to do to make a real transformational change. Here's a super-simple process that can make it easier.

To start, just allow yourself to feel whatever it is that you are feeling. Sit quietly and meditate on your feelings, using the following breathing technique.

Take a few long, deep breaths to relax your body and mind. Then, sit quietly and sense your body and any pain within it. Identify where the pain is within the body, and then place your awareness into that spot. Continue to breathe, and as you do, allow your breath to penetrate deeply into the affected area of the body. Every time you exhale, imagine your breath carrying this pain, or your fear, away with it. Imagine it actually leaving the body.

When we own our feelings, know our thoughts, and change our behaviors, we truly do begin to take charge of our reality. All three of these steps are choices we can make at any moment. We are saying for the first time that, yes, we are responsible for what we feel, say and do. We are learning to recognize that what we think determines how we feel; and in knowing this, we are empowered and become able to change our behaviors!

The choice is always our own to make.

EXERCISE
Feelings, Thoughts, and Choice

Feel whatever it is that you feel. Sit quietly and rest your mind for a few moments. Breathe and relax.

Do as you did in the preceding exercise. Identify any pain you sense within your body. Breathe into the pain you feel, exhale, and relax further with every breath. You can release pain, fear, and anxiety by acknowledging them—becoming aware of them by strengthening your present-moment awareness.

Once you are thoroughly relaxed, simply allow your awareness to touch on different thoughts that come to mind. Acknowledge any unease these thoughts bring with them. In the quiet of your mind, say: "I feel _____." Name the emotion. *For example:* anxious, angry, or sad.

Become the observer of your thoughts. And keep breathing deeply so you can support yourself to release negative feelings. As you relax, the negative emotional energy you are feeding to your brain is cut off by restorative oxygen, so your painful thoughts become muted and more isolated ... and thus observable.

Now, forgive whoever or whatever triggered the thought that made you feel uneasy. Or—and this is my favorite way— completely drop the thought. Just stop it in its tracks and release it.

Exercise continues on next page

> *Exercise continued*
>
> With practice, this technique of observing and naming your feelings will show you how your uneasy feelings originate. Then, when you can identify the source of your fears in the thoughts you hold, you can forgive yourself for allowing your ego-self to carry the burden of those types of fears and negative thoughts for as long as you have.
>
> *Forgive the past, live in the present, and feel free.*

Healthy boundaries lay the groundwork for a healthy relationship. You see, the only way to have a loving relationship with another person is through maintaining your Self-love.

If both people in a relationship have healthy boundaries, they can establish a loving connection that prevents either of them from expressing fear and less-than-loving responses to the other. In this way, the relationship either develops lovingly or ends because it is not a good fit.

Every relationship is a chance for both partners to learn and evolve.

Transformational Change: The 3Fs Approach

We must find the courage to face the past, accept it, and move on from it. There are three steps that will help you to do so and will transform your life. I call these three steps the *3Fs*. They are: feel, forgive, and foster.

To change our lives, first we must learn to *feel*, and identify the thoughts behind our feelings.

Second, we must learn how to authentically *forgive* those we have held responsible for teaching us our fear-based beliefs.

Third, we must learn to *foster* Self-love. Replacing self-doubt and self-loathing with Self-love is a powerful transformational process, which allows us to live in the present and consciously create the lives we've always desired.

These three steps can be used for the purpose of reconnecting with the all-loving, all-knowing inner Self, which helps us to transcend the physical and puts us into complete spiritual and physical alignment.

Step 1: Feel

You can begin to face the truth of your reality by feeling what you truly feel. So, as often as you can, ask, "How am I feeling?" or "How do I feel right now?"

Whenever you notice unease within yourself, name the emotions you feel for yourself, like a stream of consciousness that changes as it flows through you. The answer may be "I feel anger–pain–fear–loneliness–guilt–shame–joy–love–hope–hopelessness–uncertainty–vulnerability–anxiety…"

Once you start to observe and acknowledge whatever you are truly feeling, you'll become conscious of the positive feelings you experience AS WELL as the negative ones—positive feelings such as love, joy, contentment, confidence, and peace. You'll be able to recognize when you are having positive experiences instead of negative experiences. You won't feel as victimized by your life.

In time, you will learn to act in ways that make you feel positive—happy, joyful, content—rather than reacting in ways that cause you pain, unease, loneliness, fear, or anxiety.

Learning to feel is a very important first step in reconnecting to your inner Self. If you do nothing else, learn to reconnect with your feelings. The body is a conduit to the soul, our means to reconnect to the inner Self. And the body's purpose is to feel.

Most of us suppressed our feelings in our earlier years. We suppressed our true feelings and now, in the absence of being able to express our true feelings, we carry negative feelings. We learned to hide our feelings, deny them, or cover them up in order to keep others happy or to be accepted, valued, or loved. If you did so, then you, like me, stopped feeling and stopped trusting your instincts and inner Self. Perhaps, as happened in my case, other people's feelings became more important to you than your own. Is this true for you?

Now, if you find it difficult to connect with your feelings, you'll be glad to know that life has an amazing back-up plan you can make use of. If it's too difficult or confusing to feel what you're truly feeling, just observe your behavior instead. It can reveal a lot.

Remember, any unease we feel will prompt a reaction from our ego-self that is observable. The more we become aware of our behavior, the easier it is to recognize the feelings behind it. Thus, our unease can tell us if we are acting out of a fearful ego-self and feeling separate from our inner, all-loving Self.

Any adverse behavior or unease expressed outwardly—for instance, a judgment, a criticism, an act of aggression or anxiety, or an attack—is an observable behavior, an expression of the ego-self. When we learn to observe this behavior, we are given the opportunity to immediately recognize our feelings also, by asking right then, "How am I feeling?"

When you do this, whatever that feeling may be, simply acknowledge it. You don't have to manufacture an answer. Whatever is there is real.

Once we know how we feel, we are able to sit quietly, go within, and witness the thoughts behind the feelings we are having.

Many of us learned at some point in our lives to be afraid to face our feelings; we believed doing so made us look silly or weak. Now, it's hard to do it. Perhaps we built an ego-self-image around ourselves—presenting ourselves as rational or strong, for instance. If so, we can develop more courage by trying out the simple practice of saying to ourselves or others what we honestly feel: "I feel vulnerable," "I am feeling hurt by what you said," or "I feel lonely."

For the purpose of learning to identify your feelings at this stage, it doesn't matter what measure of neediness or attachment lies behind the feelings you have. All that matters is acknowledging "I feel lonely," "I feel sad," "I feel afraid, tired, frustrated," and so on.

Once you learn to feel, you'll be able to observe the thoughts behind your feelings.

Knowing what thoughts are behind our unease is crucial, because once we are aware of the thoughts, we have control over them. We have a choice either to keep each thought (and any unease caused by the thought) or to change it and move closer toward peace and happiness—even developing the capacity to maintain peace and happiness on a sustainable basis.

Step 2: Forgive

The next step is to learn how to forgive—authentically. Authentic forgiveness is vital to transforming the victim state because it frees us from the past and allows us to live in the present. Learning to forgive is quite a challenge, however, because the ego-self views forgiveness as a threat—*Dare I not be right?* We can only forgive once we are honest about what we are feeling and why.

Authentic forgiveness is not holding an olive branch in one hand and a stick in the other. It's not a self-righteous act designed to make ourselves feel better and another worse, or vice versa. The key to forgiveness is *forgetting*. It is learning to drop the negative thoughts associated with the person you hold responsible for the unease you are feeling, even if that person is you.

Yes, at some point we must forgive ourselves for carrying distorted teachings from the past forward in our lives for so long. It can help us to remember that these lessons of separation were passed on to us by those who had themselves received them from others. Because these beliefs are multigenerational, in the truest sense no one is to blame. This can be a life-transforming understanding.

If you need additional motivation to forgive, remember that as long as you feel separate from your inner Self you are almost guaranteed to pass on those same beliefs to your own children, if you have any, or loved ones, colleagues, or friends—an unforgiving mind will express unease, conflict, or drama for self-interest. Call it ignorance of another way. I do not wish to sugar-coat this fact for you.

Our past lessons are the distorted lessons of an unloved self, taught to us. Nothing more! The really great news, however, is that you are not genetically flawed. You are, in fact, a perfect creation living within a perfectly imperfect body for a divine purpose: to learn to love.

Our experiences in life are what they are. In the truest sense, no one is to blame. Forgiving *and forgetting* release us from the past and from the shame and guilt that cause us to react to life and others and also increase our fear. Learning to forgive *and forget* is the most powerful transformational gift you could ever consciously give yourself. It is your path to complete freedom and peace of mind, and the love and joy that accompany these.

Gerry had attended group therapy sessions for thirty years.

Forty years earlier, he'd met and married a beautiful woman. He was an alcoholic. She'd never taken a drink in her life. But she loved him. Being with an alcoholic, keeping him company, she started to drink. Ten years later, she died from the effects of alcoholism. He had been sober ever since her death. The shame, pain, and guilt he carried kept him in group therapy for the next thirty years as he helped others.

His pain was hard even for me to fathom, but I felt a real bond with Gerry. As I was unable to do it myself at the time, and knowing I could trust his judgment, I asked him, "How do you drop negative thoughts?"

He looked at me with a smile, and with two hands clenched and facing upwards, with his arms extended outwards, he simply turned his fists over and opened them.

Two years after he showed me this, I got it. Now, any time I feel uneasy, I drop it. I simply drop the negative thought, and it gives me instant peace.

In summary, when we learn to feel what we feel, it empowers us to go within and witness the thoughts behind our feelings. In time, and with practice, in the very instant we feel any unease we have the choice to change the thought that caused the emotion.

We have three options for how to handle the negative thought:

1. Drop it dead cold.

2. Replace it with a positive affirmation.

3. Be grateful for what we have in our lives, rather than what we do not.

No matter which option you utilize in any given situation, remember to make it a practice to finish by expressing gratitude for yourself and others. Also, remember that once you identify the thought, you must then forgive the person who has prompted the negative thought or belief—yourself or someone else.

Try the following exercise now to help you practice forgiveness and see if you can't turn some of the unease or pain you're currently feeling into some measure of peace or love. As you practice this technique, you may be surprised at how rapidly and efficiently you can transform pain into love and fear into peace.

EXERCISE
Dropping or Replacing Unwanted Thoughts

I invite you to bring your awareness to a time when you felt angry, upset, or in pain. Think of the occasion. Just bring it to mind.

Observe the thought, or the bearer of the unease, which is my term for the person (yourself or someone else) you hold responsible for the discomfort you are feeling.

Have you got an occasion in mind? That unease doesn't feel good at all, does it?

Once you have that scene locked and loaded mentally, close your eyes and breathe into the pain you are feeling in the body, wherever it is. As you exhale, release any negative energy you feel you can release with it.

As your body relaxes, the thought will stand out, on its own, without causing you any sensation of sickness or pain in your body.

Continue to breathe naturally, effortlessly, quietly for a few moments.

Now you are about to replace the thought you've just identified, in the hope of changing negative emotions expressed through your body into more peaceful ones.

With the thought in mind, keep your eyes closed. I'm going to ask you to simply drop it. Just drop it. After dropping it, connect with gratitude for the wonderful things in your life. Then pause for a moment and gently scan your body. Notice how dropping it has made you feel.

If, however, you found you couldn't drop the thought yet, at this point you can replace the thought with one of the positive

Exercise continues on next page

Exercise continued

and powerful affirmations below. Read them both and decide which one fits your situation best. Then, keeping your eyes closed, replace the thought.

Let's say you are thinking, "This could be hard to do..." Bring the bearer of the unease to mind: you (if you originated it) or someone else. Once you've identified the bearer, in the quiet of your mind, say:

"I love you, [Name], and accept you as you are."

Or say:

"My experiences have brought me to this place of knowing. I can now feel peace instead of pain, and I feel guided and supported."

Continue to breathe. Relax for a moment. Breathe into your diaphragm—deep into your belly. Release the thoughts and relax the body.

Open your eyes and assess how you feel. Do you feel a new level of peace?

In time, you will be able to use this simple technique and others to instantly replace any negative thoughts or feelings you experience the very moment you first become aware of them! This tool will unquestionably stop negative thoughts and emotions from spiraling out of control and stop you feeling separated from other people and reacting to your circumstances out of fear.

Step 3: Foster

Fostering Self-love and nurturing is the third step on our 3Fs path to finding complete Self-fulfillment. This step helps us become aware of the ego's limiting need to hold on to its past beliefs. The ego wants control and has unrealistic expectations about things it wants from you and others.

When we find ourselves saying, "I should have known better," but then regress to our old ways, attacking ourselves through self-loathing and self-criticism, or reacting negatively and defending ourselves to others, we should just stop, go within, and accept ourselves for messing up. The ego-self typically says, "It can't be done," "Don't be foolish," or "Life's hard." Such ideas are observable signs of self-criticism and doubt, which show that the ego is trying to stay in control. We don't have to believe what it says.

Really, you need to congratulate yourself, because each time you become aware of the uneasy feelings or negative behaviors that show you your thoughts, you are integrating new lessons that release you from the past fears that cause your unwanted thoughts, feelings, or behaviors. You are replacing an unloving reality with a loving reality—and love starts within the Self.

With these three steps, it is not a question of whether or not you *can* find peace and happiness in your life. With these three steps, you *will* find peace, happiness, and complete Self-fulfillment.

Feel what it is you're truly feeling and observe the thoughts behind those feelings. Forgive yourself and others for the experiences in your past that created those thoughts. And foster Self-love in order to change those negative thoughts.

Unless we face our past through feeling what it is we truly feel, understanding the thoughts behind our negative feelings, and forgiving ourselves and others for making us believe such thoughts, we will never understand why we think, say, and do as we do!!

We must face the past courageously, accept it—and grieve it, if we have to, so we may then move on from it in complete forgiveness.

We do not face our past to relive it, we face our past to forgive it and move on from it.

When you are aware that you have regressed to old ways of thinking and behaving, you need to give yourself lots and lots of Self-love and Self-acceptance. You must stop the doubt, loathing, and criticism you formerly indulged in, as these will prevent you from moving forward. Regression is the ego desperately hanging on!

More importantly, in the instant of applying your new-found ability to feel, forgive, and foster, know that you now have choices over your reality. In other words, you are not at the mercy of life and what happens to you—rather, you are the creator of your life.

- Any relationship can begin to mend instantly.

- Life can be enjoyed in this moment.

- Peace can be felt in the instant you choose to experience it.

- Love can be felt and expressed outwardly.

- Your past lessons can be overcome.

In any instant you choose, you can live in the present and be free! How about now? Go ahead and feel, forgive, foster, and change your life ABUNDANTLY.

CHAPTER SIX

EMPTY EARTH

*"Look deep into nature and then you will
understand everything better."*
Albert Einstein

We do not always see the beauty in life and the abundance that surrounds us in each moment. Most of us can never seem to get out of our heads long enough to enjoy it.

The way I was once living my life, I may as well have been living in a barren desert. My world wasn't real, just a continuation of the distorted perceptions I had grown up to believe were real.

We must open our hearts for change, and the mind will follow.

The fact that we experience or witness drama and conflict almost daily shows us that we are operating from minds that are not invested in Self-assuredness and Self-love, but in fear, anxiety, and doubt.

I spent much of my life living with drama and conflict, yet I didn't know the impact that drama and conflict would have on my perceptions. They impacted the way I saw life, the way I expressed love, and the way I assessed abundance or the lack of it.

I recall that after a period of some twenty years of perpetual, overzealous doing, I visited Queenstown, a quaint alpine town on the South Island of New Zealand, just by chance. I made a last-minute decision to visit this little town over another destination that had been discussed. On exiting the plane, I was instantly awestruck by its natural beauty. I connected to something I hadn't felt for many years … the earth.

Immediately, I felt incredible peace and present-moment-ness. I had an oddly overwhelming experience of feeling, "This is home." I'd never lived there—yet that was the overwhelming feeling. It was an emotional reaction to being in touch with something far greater than my mere perceptions. I stopped dead on the airport tarmac, which was surrounded by beautiful ice-covered peaks, took a moment to observe my surroundings, and breathed a sigh of relief before moving on.

I didn't understand why I felt such intense emotion—was it a complete peace that I hadn't felt for a long time? Perhaps the incredible efforts I had made for so many years had prevented my seeing the kind of beauty the earth was serving up. A pure feast of natural beauty.

I must have realized in that moment that I was so tired of the uphill battle in my life, of continually striving and wanting more— yet never looking at what was really there.

But, I'd come to realize, the thing that stopped me from seeing was the continual battle against myself.

We often fail to see the beautiful people, surroundings, and small blessings that might fill our day—we dismiss them as easily as they came. I say *fail* to see them because to see or not to see is merely a choice, and often our past determines that choice.

How can we see the abundance life offers us? How can we find more peace and love? These two questions should be our primary focus in life, *on which all other decisions are based.*

Many of us have come to believe that our entire world, or reality, is contained within the few square meters we occupy. We feel alone much of the time, each a body among many others, each fighting for what's contained in that small space, protecting and defending the reality we perceive from this state of unconscious thought.

The thoughts that create this image, and thereafter the behaviors we adopt to protect it, are what creates our fears; in turn, all protecting and defending tendencies themselves come from fear. They limit what we see to what is contained within a small physical space.

If we take a moment to become aware of our true feelings and behaviors and the thoughts behind them, we begin to expand our perception from these few square meters to a greater view of life.

Our thoughts determine who we are, and these thoughts can be based in free-flowing, love-based thoughts or, as we have learned many times through traumatic experiences, restrictive fear-based ones. Fear, unease, anxiety, and pain are the effects on our bodies when our minds are limited by our past beliefs.

All mind is intended to be free. Mind is thought, and thought is creative, and we are nature's most creative beings. What else could define creation but thought, and the power to manifest outwardly and thus to constantly evolve?

When do we take the time to look at the individual moment and see everything around us in clear sight, imagine life and love through all our senses, and embrace all life as a continuum of our own?

Only when our minds are free!

EXERCISE
Practice This Sense of Freedom

Sit for a moment in silence.

Feel any sense of unease.

Breathe into the pain you are feeling.

Relax using the breath.

Observe your negative thoughts. Forget whether you believe someone else is responsible for making you feel this way or causing you to think these thoughts.

Drop your negative thoughts. Recognize that the lessons we learned in the past are the primary cause of these negative thoughts.

Replace your painful thoughts with this affirmation: "I desire more peace, love, and joy in life." This is all about you! This is a small window of knowledge that will plant the seed for growth.

Relax, go within, breathe, and notice any new sensations of peace or freedom you experience.

If the lessons of the past could answer the riddles of life, why do so many people still feel so limited, suffer, or feel pain so often in their lives? Why are so many relationships failing and so many children having to suffer as a consequence? Why do we feel that something is always missing? Why do so many people struggle to cope, day after day, and find little rest or joy in their daily lives? And why do we perceive there to be so many problems in life?

The past has become engrained in our psyches, repeatedly—and for generations. We have come to believe that the problems we see are a normal part of life, and as a consequence they obscure so much of life.

Two Worlds: The Battle of Perception Begins

How can we take a wonderful view of life, feeling the depth of love available to us in each moment and embracing our creativity and potential to manifest the best of life, when we are consumed by the many fears we experience? It is impossible.

Is this how we wish to continue?

Think for a moment about the last time you were feeling anxious, frustrated, or concerned about something. It probably wasn't that long ago. In this state, did you feel powerlessness, anger, hurt, or abandonment—what do you recall seeing of life? I'm sure, like most, you saw more of the same negativity, and were too consumed by negative thinking to remedy your situation or make yourself feel better in some way. When this happens, life simply passes us by. Time we could spend living life is lost to poor perception, preventing us from seeing the many wonderful aspects of life and other people or feeling the positive impacts thereafter.

Think back to that last difficult occasion. What thoughts made you feel uncomfortable? Were these thoughts focused on something you were missing out on? Or how you weren't getting something you needed? Maybe your thoughts were about what someone else had—or appeared to have—that you didn't, like a new relationship, a more loving or better relationship, money, a promotion, or status? Were you fixated on what another person said or did? Maybe you were upset about not speaking up or expressing your point of view—about fitting in to please?

Most of us are consumed by thoughts that are connected to future events, or events we have very little control over. Copious amounts of time are lost thinking about our few-square-meter space and how, from that viewpoint, we think the world must operate.

Natasha spent several years concerned about the state of her marriage. By her own admission, it was not in a healthy place. After four long years of repeatedly trying to fix the marriage, she realized how much time, how much of her life, had gone by in a blink, without her connecting to life or to those she loved.

Natasha had two young daughters and was concerned about them, so she would often ask her friends, "What will happen to them? How will they feel growing up without the support of a family around them?"

For two years, she felt guilty that the marital problems she was experiencing took time away from authentically connecting with her daughters. She was overly consumed with trying to fix what she could not!

A loving, stable family for children is wonderful—it's the ideal; yet we are perfectly imperfect and going to be challenged in our lives, so we may not be able to maintain a stable family status. Acceptance of the challenges we face will always deliver a better outcome, in whatever way the situation ends.

Natasha felt she had tried everything to save the marriage; eventually, she decided to accept her situation and move on. When she knew the end of the marriage was imminent, she said, "I'm so tired of the noise." Perhaps she meant the inner noise called indecision, fighting her urges to fix an unfixable situation, the anxiety she felt ... It was a big decision for a mum with two young children.

She and her husband finally separated. Then Natasha had to accept the outcome: she was alone. It was tough at first—I'm sure it's one of the hardest decisions a couple can make. However, her changed perception and her courage in acting would change her life for the better. And while we all have some regrets at times, looking back, a decision to act, rather than a decision not to, is a choice and a journey we undertake when we "know" something needs to change.

Six months after she made the decision to separate, Natasha started to find inner peace. She began to live in the moment, and slowly but surely found a passion for living she hadn't felt for a long time.

Natasha went on to find a life purpose: assisting and empowering other women in the same unenviable position she had been in. She connected within to Self, which may only have been a survival instinct at first (an innate knowing we can turn to when things are hard), but she did it and her life has since changed considerably.

Natasha had begun to find peace of mind and joy in her life. She said her world opened up as if someone had taken off a blindfold and given her purpose. To this day, she has respect and love for her former husband, and now neither has any regrets: their separation turned into an experience that both of them gained from, and which opened up many possibilities.

Life is a journey, not a destination!

The quality of our lives is not determined by what happens to us, but rather by how well we accept what happens to us. The quicker we connect inwardly, the quicker we will know when the time for acceptance has come.

Until then, we'll be caught between old perceptions that push us to control and resist everything that happens in life—meaning that we fail to see the many splendid aspects of life—and new perceptions that encourage us to accept what happens, find the courage to act, and feel freedom and peace of mind, with eyes wide open.

EXERCISE
Exercise in Strengthening New Perceptions

Right now, what are you truly grateful for and what do you appreciate?

Do you notice the small, positive, potentially empowering things that start and end your day? Like a brisk morning walk beside the sea? The friendly people who are willing to serve you your morning coffee with a smile and a chat, the mixed and varied characters who greet you at your workplace, the smiles on your children's faces or the gift of their laughter over the silliest things, or a loved one's passion and authentic connection to you—the chance to witness the human spirit in everyday people?

Write down three things that you notice in the next three hours that please you, no matter how small.

Abundance is all around us, and to see it and appreciate it is to expand our vision. It's like training the mind in a new skill and shedding the old ones that have limited our seeing. There can be no other outcome.

Gratitude generates the power to see clearly. The loving energy in gratitude completely obscures any stifling fear-driven energy—fear dissipates when the powerful emotional energy of gratitude is expressed. This is easy to observe.

EXERCISE
Transforming Fear

Identify any fear you are experiencing and focus on it.

For example, you perceive someone as being condescending toward you.

Now, find some element of good in what you perceive, or at least accept this as an opportunity for growth.

Your perception may change instantly—for example, you may see it as a bit of harmless humor based on the other person's own insecurity, so you choose to remain friendly to them and leave no judgment on the table ... perhaps express

Exercise continues on next page

Exercise continued

it like this: "[Name] is reflecting their own sense of hurt, so it is important I avoid judging, and smile, and find inner comfort in my Self … this will benefit both of us."

Feel what it is you feel … even if it is for an instant in time.

It's easy to make excuses for the way we live and respond, when we have been taught to think the way we do. But now it's time to go beyond our limiting thoughts!

We can start with a moment in silence.

EXERCISE
A Moment for You

Try a simple exercise. Stand up, go outside, and take a deep breath. Or walk over to a window and *intently observe* all that you see.

Go and have coffee or a sandwich at your favorite café and observe people and life move around you.

Just "observe" life for this moment. Accept all that happens during this one short window of observation.

Take a moment without any thought of the normal day's proceedings, without fearing being late for a meeting or phone call, to indulge in this moment … and nothing more.

This is a moment just for you. Connect with your senses and be mindful of what is happening, like the smile on another person's face, or the taste of your coffee or sandwich.

Make a decision, for this short window, to drop (like a hot potato) all negative thought.

> Observe the peacefulness you feel in this moment! In this exercise, we need only experience the moment. Taking a moment to connect to life.

It is only from a state of conscious connection that we can truly see life for what it is and discover that we have choices. Ultimately, lessons like this will help us develop the skill of forming new habits, which will greatly benefit us and those around us.

There is benefit in having a past. Learning from it. Actually making change. In our darkest hour we rely on it to learn, unlock a door, and find the courage to walk through it.

We must, however, make sure we *do* learn from it rather than just continually springboarding from it. My past was so traumatic that I would play three different types of archetypal personalities and interchange them often. The victim. The savior trying to fix or protect others. Or the torrid persecutor ... I would utterly live life within my few square meters.

It is time to change our perceptions and become aware of such past experiences. First, to view what has occurred through heightened awareness; and second, to find the means and strength to forgive it (see my book *Silent*), and then the power and willingness to move on from it.

Our endless search for Self-fulfillment and authentic connection to life and others (all others), observable through our uneasy feelings or unruly behaviors, confirms that we have not reconnected with the inner Self. When we are able to recognize why we think, say, and do as we do, and why we react and feel so ordinary thereafter, then our perceptions begin to be questioned, and our willingness to think and act differently strengthens.

When we begin to feel something is not right within, we start to look for meaningful answers to life. We begin to ask, "Surely there must be more to life than this endless effort?" Effort that mostly leads to erratic and unsustainable rewards.

The question we face, as we stand between our past perceptions and our need to discover new perceptions, is this—do we have the courage to change?

EXERCISE
Freedom Is Detaching

Take a moment to think about the following:

Has your life turned out how you thought it would?

Are you more concerned with what others have and enjoy?

Are you grateful for who and what you have in your life or consumed by what you are doing instead?

In an ideal world, without constraints on time and money, what would your life be like? What would you be doing or not doing?

And, if you were doing what you wished, how do you think you would feel? Happy? Content? At peace? Stimulated? Satisfied?

What's stopping you from doing whatever you believe is absolutely necessary for you to be happy and content?

It is our past that is determining our present. We over-strive or feel we can't have or do the things we want. These are fear-based thoughts that live with us constantly. Either form of reasoning consumes our thoughts and distorts what we see and how we feel.

You cannot have everything on the outside just as you would like it if you don't have the necessary connection on the inside—and the courage to see everything as it really is. Most things outside us mean very little if we don't have the inner connection required to detach from them and so enjoy them.

When we can answer questions about the quality of our lives and base our answers, not on what we don't have, but on how we feel, we can then move on to recognize that, in truth, we would be sacrificing nothing, and possibly gaining everything, if we simply found the courage to feel, observe, and then act.

One "mind" (ego) is consumed by negative and restricting thoughts. It perceives a need to control life, to attach to things outside it in the hope that life will improve as a result. Unfortunately, because it never knows what it wants, it leads nowhere and keeps us confused so that truths about why we are unsatisfied lie dormant. The other "mind" (Self) categorically knows that things could be better, knows our efforts have fallen short of the mark, and unequivocally desires much more from life; seeing life for what it is it guides us to fulfilled and assured outcomes.

When the mind is conflicted, we are battling between past perceptions and inner knowledge: what we think we want versus what we really desire. Outer noise versus internal dialogue. We all desire more peace, love, and joy in our lives, and yet, due to our fears, we sabotage our chances of having them.

The dependable starting point in changing your perceptions is to apply an approach you may already be familiar with: "observe without evaluating."

In a way, observing without judging or evaluating our behaviors or thoughts, or events that occur—that is, accepting life and allowing it to unfold—is like putting our gearstick in neutral. On one side of neutrality are all the things that bring us love, joy, and peace of mind, while on the other side are all the things that cause in us feelings of shame or guilt or any form of unease.

When we are able to sit in neutral, we are allowing new perceptions to come to mind, because we are quite literally quietening our minds—allowing time to strengthen thoughts and behaviors that bring us joy and peace. We are literally watching our current reality in play. Through this simple practice, the mind will learn, over time, to gravitate to the best outcome. We just need to practice. The more we practice, the quicker and more certain will be our willingness to embrace change.

Real change takes courage, because it is emotionally very difficult for many of us to face the past or the limiting beliefs engrained in us. Saying "no more" to the distorted thinking of the past and the behaviors that inevitably follow, which have robbed us from authentically connecting to life—seeing it in high definition and full color—is a vital first step to changing our perceptions from an illusionary, fearful, limited reality to a rich, full, zestful reality.

As we transform old thoughts born from old perceptions to new thoughts born from new perceptions, our conflicted minds will require our vigilance in Self-love. This is why the simple exercise above, to "observe without evaluating," is an exceptionally effective strategy.

We can be certain that we are going to regress to old ways of thinking and behaving as we face the challenge to let go and observe. Improve a little, feel fearful of letting go, regress, observe, understand, try again—"regression with awareness."

Regression with awareness will strengthen your resolve and is fundamental to improving knowledge.

Life is challenging and our well-being is dependent on how well we perceive and accept the challenges we face. Regression to old ways of thinking and behaving—this time done with awareness of what is happening—is the only way to make lasting change.

Face Your Past and Be Free

We must face the past if we are to be free of it and live peacefully in the present. There is no other way! When we live peacefully in the present, we live without fear. Our thoughts are then born from present-moment awareness, and the mind is free to create, which allows for creative thinking.

Creative thinking leads to the realization of our heart's desires. The mind is powerful, so removing fear actually frees the mind to do what it is good at—create. Life becomes immensely enjoyable as we begin to understand we do have power over our lives and that we do have choices.

Inner Self Desires vs. Ego Wants

As we have seen many times within these chapters, there are two desires that everyone on our planet shares: the desire for love and the desire for acceptance. Ultimately, to be completely happy, we need love and acceptance, starting with Self-love and acceptance. If we do not feel love and acceptance within ourselves, we look outward to fill the void that our sense of lack creates in us. It's this sense of lack that tells us, "We can never be happy unless we have more of something: more money, more time, a better relationship, or even a better car, better kitchen, better vacation—or more days off." The list goes on and it never stops. Even anxiety can be quite addictive—it allows us to avoid rather than face.

It is true that these things can make you happy, but for how long? How long before you "need" the next "best thing"? How much will you have to work and push for it? How dissatisfied will you feel until you have it? Then you acquire something and still the lingering feelings persist. Continually pushing to maintain an image, or overcome feelings, detracts from the quality of your life—you are left forever wanting, rarely satisfied.

To transform our lives for good we need sustainable happiness rather than momentary bursts of happiness, which only foster a need to search in vain through our many attachments for a fix.

Happiness can only be felt and sustained when we choose change, look within, and begin to notice what is really important. And what is important is measured by how good something makes us feel—and whether it lasts beyond a moment in time.

The spirit of perfection—pure love—lives within us. It is real! We were all born into the world as complete, trusting, loving, creative, imaginative beings—our true being. When we separate from our true being, we feel misaligned, alone, and as if we have no foundation to life.

The mind is the creative center of all consciousness. Its conduit is the inner Self, which is one and the same as and connected to the all-knowing, all-powerful, all-loving, omnipotent, spiritual, universal energy of life.

Through our experiences we were not taught to trust in this inner Self—rather, to trust everything outside it—and so instead we created the other self ... a fear-based, thoughtless entity that is completely disconnected from our real selves. If the ego-self were really enriching and right, protective and wise, why would we still constantly feel uneasy, separate, and alone? And yet, oddly, we nevertheless find peace in the silence and stillness of some inner knowing when we reach a low ebb in life. Why? Because we are not truly an ego-self created in fear, but a spiritual, creative, powerful Self created from an incredibly loving omnipotent source.

Beautiful Earth

The reason I visited Queenstown, a small, quaint town in the Southern Hemisphere, so regularly was for its natural beauty, which seemed to transport me away from the hustle and bustle into reality, a reality that "didn't feel made up." It was a knowing, a no-ego state, and while I was there life could be genuinely observed in all its beauty. I gravitated to it—perhaps through my inner knowing? Yet I never quite realized it at the time.

In the midst of so many of life's gifts, life's blessings, I surrendered.

Attitude is a choice. What we wish to perceive is a choice. The thoughts we have are a choice! How we live life is therefore our choice!

Let's recap an earlier exercise, as it is so important in one's life when change is imminent.

A powerful driver in aligning to choice is a word we too often ignore … "gratitude." Gratitude will help you break through past constraints and remove old thinking. Why? The mind will always gravitate to the best outcome if given the chance—all we need to do is make it aware. In truth, to relearn what it already knows well!

When we are seeing life through the eyes of our fear-based ego-selves, we express fear whether or not we are being externally stimulated. No amount of external stimulus can ever satisfy the ego! Gratitude is the last thing we express when we live by the rule that *we alone can secure our own happiness, and happiness is found outside us.*

EXERCISE
What Are You Grateful For?

Take five minutes to make a list of all the things you are grateful for. Save it. Read the list from time to time, especially when you feel unhappy or discontented.

Add to the list as you become more aware of the multitude of good things in your life.

Gratitude is merely an adjustment from thinking in the past to thinking in the present, and it keeps us on track to really understanding what is important and valuable in life. It is not about what we have or who we have in our lives, but about how much we are *thankful* for what and who we have our lives.

Our gratitude, and our understanding of how all things in life are available to us in each and every minute of living, is an expression of our inner Self-connection. The more grateful we are for our lives, the better our attitudes will be, the more love we will express and receive, and the more we will see all the wonderful things that surround us and bring joy into our lives.

Learning Conscious Creation: Manifest the Life You Want

EXERCISE
Three Steps to Consciously Creating What You Desire

The *be, do, have* principle is, by my definition, the *love, peace, and joy* principle!

There are three steps to conscious creation: be, do, and have.

First, **be** the *loving thought.* Thinking of what you desire is an expression of Self.

Second, **do** what you need to do to *remain peaceful.* In other words, accept the outcome.

Third, **have** faith that the manifestation of whatever you desire is being unequivocally supported, and *be joyful about it.*

Look at the key words in each step. Here they are:

Think *loving thoughts,* regardless of what you wish to

Exercise continues on next page

Exercise continued

manifest. *Peace of mind* becomes the guide that you are holding true to the desire. *Enjoying the moment* means not allowing your fears to interfere in the process!

In summary: use your greatest desires—the desires for love, peace, and joy—to attain whatever it is in life that you wish for.

Whatever we desire must come from our truest, most important, universal desires of love, peace, and joy. Life abundance involves manifesting or consciously creating everything we desire! If you want more love, send more love. More money? ... What would that money do? Be the loving thought behind the money, not just wanting money in order to feel better about yourself.

Unless we connect within to the source of pure love and acceptance, we cannot consciously create what we desire, because quite simply we will not know what our desires are; instead, we will believe that our endless wanting will ultimately lead to life abundance.

In any reality, to enact the law of conscious creation, you must *be* it (whatever "it" is) before you *receive* it. If you want more love, or anything stemming from this basic desire, then *hold a loving thought* in your mind, and replace your fears of not having love (or whatever it is you desire) with new, loved-based thoughts.

Next, *do* the things you would do if you already had what you desire. Knowing that negative thoughts will block the creation, drop them as you become aware of them, and allow yourself to feel and *remain peaceful* about your desired manifestation.

Finally, with great conviction and faith, know you have it. Allow yourself to experience in advance the same *joy* you will feel once your desired outcome has materialized tangibly in the world.

Learn to apply the **be** (loving thoughts), **do** (peace of mind), **have** (remaining joyful) approach to any desire. In this way, you are learning to enhance the quality of your life from a love-based reality.

Rich, Full Earth

See the smile on someone's face, hear the laughter of children, teach your loved ones to connect within and trust in their instincts and creative abilities, feel the caress of a loved one. Smell the salt air and use your senses to feel life.

Give more of yourself to others because it will make them happy. As you do these things, your inner Self is awakened.

You will feel the richness of life, and the effects will positively affirm your actions ... you will feel peace of mind.

The more we share our Self, the more joy we experience in life. As we connect to the Self, we begin to see the world as loving, abundant, and full of vitality. Outside pressures lose their grip over us.

Our new perception is what changes the world we see into a full, vibrant, abundant, and loving earth. Live in the present and create more of the same. Reconnect to life and life must serve you more joy and peace.

Life has so much to offer us, yet we often fail to see it. Its abundance is available to us in each and every moment ... not before or after it. When we begin to identify what is holding us back from seeing a rich, full earth, our minds may become conflicted between our past beliefs (holding on) and our new beliefs (letting go). The reason for this is quite simple: we have become so fixated on how life "should" be that we actually can't believe there is an alternative.

We each desire peace and joy; it is the natural inheritance of who we truly are. The gifts of peace and joy reside at the core of our being. We need to connect to this knowing, to turn the cycle of negativity we have lived with for years into a cycle of positivity. It is done at the instant of our choosing to know—we recognize it through our feelings!

Once we are aware that resisting life and our life experiences is futile—and only adds to the level of unease we feel, obscuring our view of the many wonderful gifts available to us—we begin to seek different perceptions and possibilities in our world.

We have the power to change our perceptions, and thereby change the thoughts and behaviors that follow them. Yes, at first the mind will be conflicted between old and new, but we have an inbuilt guide that we can learn to harness and follow. This internal guide will ultimately transform our lives by clearing our vision and unlocking our inherent ability to perceive the rich, full earth we were given.

CHAPTER SEVEN

UNMALICE CURSE

*"I am slowly learning that some people are not good
for me, no matter how much I love them."*
WisdomQuotes

An *unmalice curse* is the pain and trauma we can experience; more often than not, it stems from someone else's unintentional ignorance, resulting from their past lessons, rather than through any intention to inflict trauma. They burden us with their beliefs, and these beliefs become our own. Lessons passed on, passed down through generations or spread through society.

Yet in those lessons, our greatest opportunity awaits ... These are lessons that provide our motivation to uncover the truth, move past our many fears, and seek knowledge that will greatly enhance our life.

An unmalice curse, we could therefore conclude, is a manifestation of creation's perfectly imperfect plan—it powers our quest to give our lives immeasurable meaning and purpose.

I grew up believing I was not good enough, and thought that the way I could feel good about myself, and prove to myself that I was in fact worthy, was by hiding my lack of self-worth. We all have a choice of path when things feel bad— fight or flight. Mine was the former. Those who suffer trauma in whatever form express their hurt in any number of ways. I would express a compulsion to succeed at all costs; I became judgmental and overly defensive, my insecurity buried deep within, fueling the determination I felt. Workaholism, rather than any other drug of choice—that was just the way the cards were dealt. But early experiences stayed with me— they became the way I viewed life and communicated with people.

Tunnel vision and overzealous behaviors prevented me from seeing any other possibility. My life, as enriching as it may have appeared from the outside, was in fact limited in so many ways. Authentic relationships outside working life were sacrificed, there was little to no time to smell the roses, and those I said I loved I burdened with an obsessive "do all, be all" attitude. There was almost no life balance.

Generally, we all see ourselves as loving, although we express ourselves in ways that are anything but—often not by choice but through misunderstanding. Here, the unmalice curse is repeated. We fail to recognize these fears that make up our psychology and act out our lessons unaware of their detrimental impact on ourselves and others. We see ourselves as good or loving yet misunderstood. Our characters butt heads with those of others who feel equally misunderstood—each projecting hurt and pain through control or manipulation, each desperate to have their needs met—the fear-based need to fix our past beliefs about ourselves. We then attract into our lives those who give us the greatest opportunity to evolve—in essence, by exposing the lessons of fear we learned, buried deep within, and carried for so long.

In other words, we express ourselves in the manner that repeats our past and pass on the same fears we learned, often not from malice but unintentionally.

We express love from the ego-self (see the chapter "Shallow Love"). Our intention to be understood and loved is often clouded by the negative thoughts and behaviors we project because of how we have come to believe life should be for us.

Those of us who never felt we had control when we were growing up go through life seeking out answers to the questions that were left unanswered:

- How do I manage the external stuff?

- How do I find and sustain happiness and peace?

- How can I find a stable and loving relationship?

What we don't seem to ask is—why? In short, the past is hidden from view. "*Why* don't I manage the external stuff appropriately?" becomes a subliminal question.

These questions form the basis of our unease and can be identified through our repetitive thoughts and reactive behaviors. We play out the drama, or we watch it being played out all around us, often experiencing relief that we aren't alone in our thinking.

We learned to stop listening to the internal messages—SELF-LOVE AND TRUST—that we could have relied on as a constant means of guidance, which would have given us the vital inner confidence to accept life and an innate knowledge of how to deal with it. It would also have given us gratitude for our efforts, what we achieve, and how we communicate, instead of the distorted reality we have chosen to be consumed by. Inner confidence stops the blame game; it allows us to take responsible action when life throws challenges our way; and it leaves us ample energy to detach from any rigid beliefs and enjoy more abstract thinking and zest for life. Ample energy to simply enjoy life, to enjoy people from all walks of life and its many pleasures.

The generational patterns of those who knew no better were ingrained in us—layer upon layer of conditioning that inevitably broke down the innate knowledge of Self-love and trust we were born with.

Ignoring the voice of wisdom within—nature's gift—leaves us reliant on sources outside us for the happiness we seek and deserve! The wisdom we gain from opening our eyes to these past experiences, and why they occurred, is life-transforming and liberating.

Of course, it is not only the family that creates a child's distorted beliefs. There are also a child's caretakers in schools, influential figures in the workplace or society, and our culture at large—the way society normalizes certain characteristics and relationships. In fact, anyone in authority or in an influential position who we have come to rely on or be mentored by can impact how we view ourselves. Learning has the potential to distort our thinking, just as learning has the potential to improve it. Is it malice? Often not!

Regardless of how we express or project the fear-based lessons we learned, if we continue to do so, without awareness, we will continue to pass on the same lessons to others, and the cycle will continue, leaving many feeling unsure and alone … leadership will be lost.

My parents were rarely seen in our home. Both worked religiously and indulged their habits extensively. They pursued their work and social agenda in the manner they wanted. And in hindsight, I'm sure, they would feel remorse for their own actions or a sense of guilt. They would see their actions as stemming from the limited mindset that was passed on to them. Their actions and reactions were a necessity in their extremely limited view of reality—they knew no better: I came to learn, years later, that trauma was inflicted on them when they were young.

They simply demonstrated visceral behaviors based on their own inner fears about love and life. They too, perhaps, believed that all would be lost if there was any deviation from their rigid approach, or perhaps their thoughts and actions prevented them from facing their truths. Maybe it was as simple for them as not believing or trusting sufficiently in love, or believing that love would provide the answers they were seeking.

As children, my siblings and I were left to try to put the pieces of our lives together. We later saw our relationships as important, yet conditional: important because, having lacked nurturing feelings of love while growing up, we had an intense (yet unstable) desire for it; and conditional because we had come to believe that relationships must be difficult and challenging. This reasoning wouldn't lay the groundwork for healthy relationships, would it? What it could do was lay the foundation for the expression of neediness and reactive intimacy (into-me-u-see). But don't look too close!

We went on to ingrain the lessons in shallow love we learned. Our intimate relationships most certainly became our greatest lessons in life and, further, a primary catalyst for change.

But here is the important takeaway … it is meant to be exactly as it is—it is our most important journey, our soul evolution … and our greatest opportunity to find an incredibly beautiful, inspiring freedom and plentiful reality.

When we hold on to fear-based thinking, with no real mentor in Self, we will embed ourselves into our past beliefs, and rely so heavily on retaining those beliefs that any threat or disparagement of them can feel like a life and death issue. That is how we view the lessons we learned—as all too important.

Our ego-self will act in ways that attract to it those people who will offer us our greatest awareness.

"There are no failed relationships. Every person who enters and exits your life does so in a mutual sharing of life's divine lessons."
Wayne Dyer

Our ego-self attempts to disguise the fears we live with, afraid that if we become aware that we are responsible for the unease we feel, we might begin to question all the beliefs that have guided us for much of our lives. Taking responsibility for what we think, say, and do is something we are afraid of—it is far easier to blame or judge others and hold our little world in place with all its crammed, misguided distortions.

Only we can change our thoughts, our beliefs, and our behaviors … no one else can, no matter what we think. We are each ultimately responsible for our peace of mind, the joy or happiness we feel in any moment, and we can make the decision to enjoy them at any time we choose—we just need to know why we feel the way we do, and how to change it.

In truth, stopping the "unmalice curse" starts and ends with YOU.

As long as we remain unaware of this truth—that we are solely responsible for our own happiness—we will react all too easily to others, blame others for our feelings, persistently justify and defend our behaviors, seek out attachments to people and things to relieve us of our burdens, and continually project our pain and unease outwardly.

Deep within, we believe we have good intentions, and so when our shallowest perceptions of ourselves are questioned, we react all too easily. Feeling misunderstood, invalidated, unloved and supported, we readily defend our reactions. This protective mechanism holds our reality in place. What we are not doing is asking ourselves,

"Why am I doing this and how do I change?" Instead, we seem to persist with unease, hurt, anxiety, or pain without questioning it.

Of course, like us, others often cannot see past their own needs and wants; they cannot understand our reasons for behaving the way we do. They, like us, do not hear our cries for love, because they are equally consumed in defending their own self-images, which, like ours, were constructed in the absence of Self-love.

The really good news is that any relationship can be revived when the mind starts to believe it has choices!

Our purpose in life is to recognize that our past experiences were, for the most part, not inflicted on us by design, or at worst were an outburst or expression of another person's unloved self. If we do not see this then the pain and trauma we feel and continue to carry will prevent us from living life joyfully or graciously.

You see, it is awareness that transmutes the pain and unease by allowing us to recognize that the lessons we learned and then acted on were not our fault. In this recognition, we begin to stop the self-hate, self-loathing, self-criticism, self-sabotage ... and instead plant the seeds of change—change that will lead to growth (knowledge).

To transform our lives and remedy the past, we must forgive ourselves for blindly carrying the lessons from our past and behaving in ways that were harmful and painful to us and others. These were errors based on the unmalicious (that is, for the most part unintentional) teachings of others. We must forgive others for their part, accept we carried these lessons, and learn to forgive our (ego)self for doing so. We knew no better—let's find the power to forgive self and others. This is one of the hardest undertakings in life, because it is hard to face the past and equally hard to forgive it. Yet when we do, miracles beyond anything we can currently imagine will occur!

We are relational beings and enhance our lives through relationships. The harder the relationship, the more willing we become to look at ourselves for answers, and over time it will be relationships that lead us to a crossroad ... that vital and integral moment for change.

At some point, fearful beliefs will no longer be able to hold our limited reality in place. Why? Because we are creative spiritual beings by nature and cannot be limited!

The simplest and most effective means of escaping the past and living freely in the present ... is contained in the power of forgiveness (see the 3Fs in the previous chapter).

There is little inner silence in the environment we witness daily; we seem to have no time to question our own reality, while nonetheless steadfastly observing that of others—comparisons are all too easy to make, and they sow seeds of discontent.

Our unease and anxiety are reflected in our actions. Our past has determined our reality and it is this we must face if we wish to discover a new, more desirable reality and the many benefits that come from it.

Let's apply two practices that can significantly change our lives.

EXERCISE
A Simple Meditation—the Beginning of Awareness!

Use this meditation whenever you feel any measure of unease. Take the unease as a sign that you are hanging on to thoughts and beliefs based on your learned experiences. In other words, if unease arises it may be a sign that you haven't forgiven yourself or someone else for the way you feel.

This exercise is also a wonderful way to start or end your day.

Begin by sitting quietly.

Breathe deeply into your chest and diaphragm. Focus your awareness on your breath until your body starts to relax.

Breathe consciously—that is, observe the breath for as long as you can. If you feel agitated when you sit quietly, merely observe the anxiety and stay with the meditation.

Continue to breathe deeply into the diaphragm. Once you feel your body relax, allow your mind to release all thoughts.

Of course, your mind will not go entirely blank, and often this process will heighten your awareness of your thoughts—

Exercise continues on next page

Exercise continued

often, thoughts immersed in the fears you carry.

As thoughts come to mind, let your awareness move to each new thought and then repeat the breathing and releasing process.

At some point, you will get a moment of silence—you will discover what it is like to enjoy a blissful inner state. Only a few moments is enough to trigger awareness. Perhaps at first, given that so many of us have become dependent on feelings of anxiety, you may not easily accept these new feelings—so daily practice is very important.

You may also make a conscious decision to drop each negative thought or replace the negative thought with a positive affirmation, such as this: "I am at peace. I desire peace, and I can have peace, because my past is my past and I forgive all within it."

This is very powerful when thoughts consume your meditation time—and it's perfectly fine to use a positive affirmation as a mantra. Prayer is another powerful practice, and if you are used to saying prayers—use them. There are no rules in meditation other than to practice often—it makes room for a blissful life balance.

Once again breathe, until the mind relaxes.

No matter which approach you take—breathing, dropping the thought, or replacing the thought with an affirmation or prayer—rather than choosing to fear, just know that everything will turn out well for you. Allow yourself to begin to trust in this—stick with it.

Spend a few peaceful moments in silence with eyes closed.

Open your eyes and for five minutes sit quietly, observe life around you—simply observe everything.

Observe how you feel—then go about your day.

The more often you practice meditation, the more access you will have to inner peace when you need it. In reality, we all need an escape valve—a reliance on inner Self. Especially while we are learning how to sustain a balanced and fulfilled life—to manifest more love, communicate more authentically, forgive and forget so as to free ourselves from past afflictions, and live freely in the present.

Practice regularly, just for ten minutes or so whenever you remember to do so or need a way out of some challenging emotion—anxiety, stress, unease of any kind, or feelings of hopelessness, helplessness, insecurity, or uncertainty.

Although I very much enjoy longer practice periods, the reason I also do shorter ones is that I learned early on that meditation manages the afflictions of anxiety and negative thinking exceptionally well, and also clears the mind, making it easier to answer any challenging questions.

When the mind is free of fear, it will only operate from a loved-based state, and any thought that comes from a love-based state will be one we can rely on.

You can meditate anywhere—in any comfy chair, or in the front seat of your stationary car (this can be an exceptionally wonderful opportunity, when cocooned in the warmth and quiet of your vehicle). Or in a few moments stolen from your working day (this can really help your day go well), or in a park (sit for several minutes and simply observe nature ... then close your eyes, breathe, and begin).

It doesn't matter how many times you meditate, or where you do it ... find the seconds, minutes, to achieve inner Self-connection, and learn of its vast benefits.

The more you practice, the less stressed you'll feel, and the more resilient and confident in Self you'll become, and the more willing you will be to move out of the past and into the peaceful present.

Meditation helps with anxiety because it has the power to calm the mind and give a moment of reprieve, allowing us to realign our focus inward rather than outward.

Living with anxiety involves denying one's reality, preferring instead to keep the past alive within. We all live with anxiety to some degree in our lives, and the impact can become quite severe, especially in young people. We seem not to be able to get out of our heads to find peace. Sometimes our anxiety is an excuse or permission to avoid facing why we feel so "ordinary"—it is a competitive world where comparisons with others have become all-important.

Anxiety is damaging to our society. It keeps the mind locked in a vortex of negativity and denies us the chance to know why. Searching for the right answers becomes irrelevant—finding an answer that fits a distorted mindset seems far more important. The reason any answer will do is because a mind afflicted with this constant emotion is never at peace—so the answer cannot satisfy the question—ever!

Anxiety fuels more anxiety, until it becomes a torrent of misguided thoughts, each adding fuel to the next. Physically, it can bring an adrenaline rush where the mind grapples for a solution; however, in this state we can rarely find any reliable solution. Finding ourselves unfulfilled, we try to compensate. We need more and more stimulation to maintain our defenses. We look to others for validation, and highly prize the like-minded individuals we find—anything to keep our beliefs in tow.

The way to gain freedom from this pattern is to recognize anxiety as an adapted emotion we learned from the effects of continued separation from a sustainable source: our inner Self.

Meditation will start the process of awareness; forgiveness will take that awareness and transmute it into a Self-possessed freedom, giving you the power to manifest the life you most desire!

The antidote, and cure, to our unease and its dramatic effects on our life is the *indelible power of awareness and forgiveness*!

EXERCISE
Forgiveness—A Driving Force for
Real and Sustainable Change!

1. Our willingness to forgive ourselves for carrying the shame of our past lessons is essential in the process of moving past the past.

2. Accepting our behaviors and recognizing that they were nothing more than mistakes, but taking responsibility for them, is a necessary step. *No one is responsible for what you do or how you feel but you!*

> 3. Also vital is forgiveness of those we viewed as responsible for the lessons we learned—taking responsibility for how we feel is the key to living freely in the present.
>
> True forgiveness is not holding an olive branch in one hand and a stick in the other—true forgiveness means forgiving and forgetting! Drop any negative thoughts. It does not mean that you must stay within a relationship or an environment if it does not suit you; it merely means drop the negative thoughts, move past the anxiety by creating a stable foundation for an alternative thought process, and almost instantly feel a real sense of peace of mind—there is NO other way.

Yes, certain things others do and say are going to hurt us. But the longer we let these things negatively impact us, the more power we give to the negative energy that fuels our anxiety, limiting our ability to see a way out and stopping us from taking back control (real control) over our life.

The ego-self is not in control in the true sense; in fact, more often than not it is out of control.

We can live life thoughtlessly and unconsciously—or mindfully and consciously by recognizing the simple premise "we must each take responsibility for our life."

We teach our children the same lessons we were taught. We teach them conditional love, the inability to trust in the Self, and the inability to take responsibility for their actions, forgive, or feel free. The unmalice curse is passed on to them—again, through ignorance more than anything else. We often harm others unintentionally. When we are aware of these teachings we pass along to others—including to those we deeply love and value—we can find the motivation to shift our perception from the discomfort we live in to the peace and joy we desire for ourselves and those we say we love.

It isn't easy to face our false beliefs and change, yet we are completely capable of it when we choose not to accept any longer the pain and suffering we witness, endure, and normalize—when we decide to follow our hearts, and to teach others new lessons in the way we approach life and other people. In this way, we can give others the skills to also change course—to feel empowered to follow suit—with everyone benefiting from one another and the new-found lessons we encapsulate in our lives.

It is the greatest gift we can give. Let that gift fuel our own desire for real change.

EXERCISE
A Day of Forgiveness

Try authentic forgiveness for just one day—make a promise to yourself you will try this!

1. Forgive yourself, your neighbor, your friends, your significant other, your children, your parents, your business partner, the person in the street who didn't smile at you, and the person in the car who just blasted you with his horn.

2. Just forgive, from first thing in the morning—no matter what happens when you wake, or what is said, or what didn't work out. Just observe without evaluating; forgiveness is the goal—distance yourself from any reaction until you have taken a moment to think about the promise you made to yourself.

3. Do not allow yourself to harbor resentment or negative thoughts of any kind—drop it.

This exercise takes vigilance, keen awareness throughout the day to stay the course. Stay with it no matter what challenges you face—accept no excuses for breaking your promise!

At the day's end, sit quietly for a moment, breathe consciously, and allow your mind to run through the day's events. What occurred, and how did you manage your day differently? What were the effects on you? Did people respond to you differently, and did you feel more relaxed and at peace?

This is about recognizing at the day's end "how you feel," how much you got done without the fanfare and drama, or

---

how the anxiety you might normally feel was greatly reduced. Reflect on your day and discover how productive it was.

Once you've mentally noted a few discoveries, sit with this awareness for a few moments. Go to the breath, exhale and inhale, close out all thought, and feel the pleasure that arises.

It is in forgiveness that you connect to life. Once you have forgiven, reaction is replaced with responsible action. Anxiety no longer keeps you stuck in the prison of your mind.

Forgiveness means you no longer host an inner dialogue consumed by past lessons and are free to live in the present, experiencing new thoughts based on new perceptions: in other words, you can think creative thoughts that inspire peace and love in each moment of choosing, allowing you to authentically connect to others, build your inner strength (willingness) and confidence, remove negative thoughts, and live freely in the moment.

Forgive the past, and the past no longer has control over your thoughts!

The greatest lesson we can teach others, including those we love, is the importance of the will to genuinely forgive. And to genuinely forgive is to move on ... literally to forget. You will often hear people who feel persecuted ask, "How can I forget?" or say, "I would forgive them if they apologized first." There are many ways we use the olive branch to disguise the stick behind our back; however, it is the stick that causes the harm to ourselves. The self-harm that closes the door on change.

On the path to healing past beliefs, we need to access forgiveness often. Choosing this path is choosing a path to Self-love, which gives us the ability to love others genuinely and unconditionally.

Forgiveness is your loving defense against a world in crisis. Forgiveness will transform a loathing self to a loving Self, a fearful self to a fearless Self, a doubtful self to a knowing Self, a hopeless world to a hopeful world, a thoughtless reality to a thoughtful reality.

Forgiveness is the bridge between the outer world and the inner world and it has the power to balance the physical and the spiritual within us, creating harmony.

Don't take my word for it. Try it for yourself! Forgiveness paves the way to sustaining a conscious mind, which is the greatest gift we can give ourselves and those we love.

A Conscious Mind is the Greatest Gift We Can Give

Have you ever been in a situation with a crowd of people you barely know and just listened to their conversations? Listened to the pain and drama people express in everyday conversation when they describe the events that are impacting their lives?

To recognize the thoughts of our unloved self and face up to them, we must be vigilant in identifying our feelings. While learning to understand our feelings, we also learn to recognize the origins of the limiting beliefs that cause our unease and pain. From recognizing our feelings, the process goes like this:

1. Observation of feelings—or, if we can't identify the feeling, observation of our behaviors

2. Awareness of the thought behind the feeling …
   choosing to delve deeper, to the origin of the thought (acknowledging the past lesson)

3. Boring down into the lesson (often hard to do, and sometimes professional help is required here)

4. Forgiveness

5. Release

An observation to note here—for some, it is impossible to get to the origin of the thought without experiencing considerable pain. If you can, invest in professional help at this point, and if the pain is too great then stop. Time is on your side.

When we choose the path of Self-love, we are able to communicate authentically with Self, and subsequently with others—free of the limiting, unforgiving thoughts that have held us prisoner to our minds for so long. Expression of a loving Self is inevitably acknowledged and returned in kind—give yourself time.

Regardless of the circumstances we have lived through and the conditions that were placed on the love we experienced, we can forgive and live freely in the present at any moment we choose. The inner Self is the only thing we will express outwardly! Can it be done instantly? Yes. However, the task of maintaining it, no— at least, not normally. We typically relapse into past behaviors and limiting thoughts as we unravel the many distorted layers we've built up through our lives.

Forgive yourself, and then all others, in relation to your past experiences; recognize them as an unmalice curse—nothing more. As hard as that may be, realize you're choosing to be free and to manifest a bountiful life. This is the only way it can be done.

In many cases, we have become limited only by the choices we have made, and nothing more—our lack of awareness has prevented us from seeing more in life. In other cases, sadly, we do lack an entirely free choice. But doesn't that mean we have more of a duty to Self to recognize the choices we *do* have, when they are available?

We cannot have the experiences we wish for above all else when we are disconnected from the Self and from life. If we cannot love the Self, we cannot give love. Fortunately, we are free to enjoy an unlimited abundance of love and joy, save for our own fears. Self-love unravels those fears, allows us to access that abundance!

Everyone desires love and acceptance. Ultimately, life is all about love and acceptance. Forgiveness is the method by which our physical forms can know love, express love, and receive love instantly. Yet we too easily ignore the power of forgiveness, preferring instead to believe that our reality is not ours to choose.

We hold on to resentment or unresolved anger for far too long. Identifying the truth behind our lives eliminates this anger. We must learn to forgive the ego-self, which has kept us in the fear-based reality we witness each day, and nurture ourselves through this period.

It is time to face our truth, meditate, become aware, and practice forgiveness, at every opportunity until it becomes a habitual practice. We need to understand that our reality is ours and we are each solely responsible for it.

Let's close this chapter with two highly powerful meditations. One will delve into the deep recesses of your mind and ask questions to help you unravel why you have felt so limited; the second is a short, powerful meditation in forgiveness that can be applied anytime you have been triggered into a reaction or poor behavior that has not served you well, to enable you to find peace instead.

EXERCISE
Boring Down—Deep Awareness Meditation Practice

Uncovering the Truth

When you feel your mood dip, or when you feel fear come over you, stop and reflect.

1. Ask yourself in this moment of unease … **how do I feel?** Identify what you feel … verbalize it. I am angry, I am worried, I am feeling unloved, I am feeling needy, I am feeling scared, unhappy, hopeless, unsafe and so on.

2. Sit quietly, breathe deeply six or seven times or more …

3. Bring up the feeling again, verbalize it if you need to … but get it out. It is very important that you take this moment of you-time, to end the negative feelings; if you don't, it will be detrimental to your day.

4. Ask yourself … **what has made me feel like this?**

5. Clearly identify the interaction or event that caused you to feel the way you do. Perhaps you found yourself shifting from happiness to worry in a moment—what triggered it? (Growing up, from a very young age, I would never know when the family home would turn from laughter to violence … from humor to abuse. Through life, I came to realize that any happiness I experienced would readily dissipate at the thought of my roller-coaster past, where many happy moments turned sour in an instant. I'd find myself worrying and wondering, "When is it going to go wrong?")

6. Now ask yourself questions like, "Is what I'm feeling justified?" and "Am I overreacting?"

7. *Sit quietly, breathe, clear the mind for as long as you can, and now with courage bore down to a period in your earlier life when you felt the same feelings.*

8. Drill down as far as you can, even remembering your earliest childhood memory. Try to discover what part of your past has caused this feeling in you. When you expose the truth of the past, it begins to lose its grip over you.

9. Ponder for a few moments; if nothing comes to mind or you are unwilling to look, try again another time.

10. Do not leave the meditation like this! Now, let all thoughts go, continuing to inhale and exhale, and when you feel sufficiently relaxed, sit quietly for a few more minutes. If a thought comes, let it go; simply return to your peace of mind. Enjoy the silence.

11. Open your eyes, observe everything around you, listen to all sounds, relax into the moment. End the meditation.

Your path to sustainable peace and joy in your life begins with awareness and ends with forgiveness.

If you feel the need to express your feelings and your new awarenesses to people you love, and you explain to them what you are doing, allowing yourself to be vulnerable, you may be surprised how much your loved ones appreciate seeing a side of you they haven't seen before.

EXERCISE
Forgiveness—Meditation Practice

If you notice that you're holding on to anger or blame for any pain you feel, and you find it challenging to bore down, continue with this simple and highly effective step.

1. Begin by observing your feelings. It is very important that you take this moment of you-time, to end the negative feelings; if you don't, it will be detrimental to your day once again. It could be a person or an event that you are holding responsible for the pain you feel. (Sometimes this person may be yourself—as I explained in my personal story above—but you may have been triggered by the blame you now attach to someone else—in this realization, find your release.)

2. Once an event or person comes to mind, close your eyes and breathe into the pain you are feeling. Notice specifically where the pain is located in the body and breathe into that location. As you exhale, allow the negative energy to be released with your breath.

3. Continue to breathe. Do so effortlessly and quietly for a few moments.

4. From here we are about to replace the thought and change any negative feeling. It's wonderful to have the awareness you will gain through this practice to call on whenever you need it.

5. What thought occurred that made you feel so bad?

6. With the thought in mind, keep your eyes closed. I'm going to ask you to simply drop it—JUST DROP IT! Drop the negative thought. Let it go!

7. Now breathe—consciously, several times.

Notice how dropping the thought made you feel!

Or, if you cannot drop the thought, replace the thought with one of the following positive and powerful affirmations. While holding the person or event that has prompted your unease in mind, think or say:

"I love you, [Name], and accept you as you are."

"This experience has brought me to a point in my life where I can make significant changes and feel peace instead of pain."

8. Return to the breath, let all negative feelings go, and when you're ready open your eyes and go about your day.

If you felt a level of peace from practicing this forgiveness meditation, it is because you connected to your inner Self, free of responses that were conditioned by the past. You controlled the outcome because the control came from your inner Self and was not reliant on some other person or event.

You took control of your thoughts, and those thoughts were liberated through forgiveness.

Once you have practiced these exercises several times, you will begin to realize the power you hold over your mind and become able to access peace of mind more and more readily.

By holding on to your peace of mind, you are simultaneously letting go of negative thoughts that originated in the past, thereby allowing your Self to live freely in the present.

It is through these practices that you can put an end to the unmalice curse, empowering the mind and allowing yourself the freedom to discover how much power you really do have in determining every aspect of your life.

CHAPTER EIGHT

JUDGING IS A TRAP

"Good judgments will often draw their wisdom from poor ones."
Author unknown

Helpful Judgment vs. Unhelpful Judgment

Releasing judgment of others is actually releasing judgment of yourself.

There are two kinds of judgment. The first is judgment based on logical reasoning, such as judging who, for example, would be the best person to play on your sports team at an upcoming event, or who would be best to tackle a particular role in your office. At those times you're judging, "What is the best course of action to take?" Not all judgments are bad. A helpful or healthy judgment helps you decide what to do to preserve your peace of mind, how not to lose your money, how to keep yourself safe, how to act responsibly, how to improve quality of life for yourself and those you care for, how to set a healthy boundary for someone who negatively impacts your life, what you need to do to make your life easier, what you should do to improve your relationships, how to make healthy changes, and so on. These forms of judgments connect people and ideas—they involve common goals and expand consciousness.

Judgments of the second kind, those I'm focusing on here, relate to our limited and limiting beliefs. These detrimental judgments are based on negative perceptions we've held about life based on what we've witnessed and experienced. They have a negative impact on our world because they uphold, if not further expand, the many distorted perceptions we have of ourselves, and as a consequence our lives and the people within them.

Poor perceptions lead to unhelpful judgments. Poor judgment is an unwillingness to look beyond our limited beliefs and thought process. Our need to judge can trap our minds in a spiral of negativity, keeping us separate from life and other people, detracting from the quality of our relationships, and robbing us of our peace of mind.

We are focusing here on these detrimental judgments in the hope that, through recognition of the impact these judgments have on us and those around us, we will learn to judge differently.

A misperception may create erratic behavior, the thought and the behavior intertwined and descending into a spiral of negativity. This negativity fuels our anxieties and sense of unease. Judging hinders our willingness to reason—it produces opinions fixed by their own distorted beliefs. The separation that judging creates (separation between ego-self and others, or ego-self and life) maintains our belief that we must be (ego-)self-reliant to survive—it robs us of any faith in our inner Self-knowing and is the cause of much of our fear. In most cases, it stems from what we are most afraid of ... the unknown, or the lack of a sustainable base or supporting structure in our life.

Judgments prevent creative solutions that heal our unease, and they stop us from seeing that any other possibility exists. They make us feel we're powerless and, worse, victims of life.

If we become aware, we can start to notice each judgment's detrimental impact—notice how this unforgiving approach reflects our own unresolved anger, anxiety, near-constant unease, self-doubt, and sense of lack.

Judgments can range from something as simple as reacting negatively to a slow vehicle on the road in front of us to forming an opinion based on someone's clothing or hairstyle, their religious denomination, the color of their skin, their ethnicity or nationality, their education or fortunes in life, or their behavior or language. We may even judge the weather, blaming it for how we feel! We may judge our colleagues, partners, spouses, and relationships whenever things don't seem to go our way.

In this world, nothing escapes our judgment. As you read this book, my hope is that you will become aware of how often we do judge ... a simple review will, I'm certain, confirm this fact. The frequency may surprise you.

Subconsciously, we expect our judgments, like all ego traits, to provide some sort of comfort, but in truth they prevent us from any relief other than the shallow laughter they may provoke: validation from like-minded others will be the ego's only comfort here.

Let me give a quick example. Let's say we judge someone in a room as being "boastful" or "too loud." We may expect others to laugh along or agree with us. In other words, we may hope to boost our image by judging the other person, perhaps feeling insecure that they focus attention away from us—or perhaps feeling a need for reassurance that we, by contrast, communicate appropriately.

This may give us a sense of validation for a moment: a happy feeling; yet this feeling either cannot last or will create distance or attract criticism and cause us some level of concern.

At some point the judge (the ego-self) becomes judged, according to the same sensitivities and fear by which we expressed ourselves. Fear, expressed as a judgment, is not resolved—in judging, we are only creating more of the same, leaving ourselves hypervigilant against anyone judging us in turn. Fear begets fear. How easily our images of ourselves seem under threat; how easily we become defensive, and react.

The foundation on which we build our home will determine its strength and durability!

When we judge, we must be prepared to live by the judgments we make, because when we judge we set ourselves apart from others – and will have that cross to bear, easily becoming defensive about those very aspects of ourselves that we do not accept in others.

As long as we ignore the negative emotional impact that judging has on us, we may think that we are free to judge without consequence.

While many people had far better personal relationships than I allowed myself to enjoy for many years, relationships were secondary to my definition of success—success was instead the fact that I could go anywhere and buy virtually anything I chose. I judged all of life by the same standard.

It was a standard that I believed others should also strive toward. My many relationships were based around a priority list, a list my ego developed as I was growing up, of things I believed would give meaning to my life—material success first, then relationships. As for a work–life balance? Nowhere to be seen.

If others were having difficulty with their relationships because of overworking, I judged their relationships in the manner I had been taught. I had a belief that relationships were challenging at the best of times, and that material success was all-important. I would support people's drive for success more than I would maintain any empathy toward personal relationships.

In holding this view, I was making an error in judgment, the effects of which I would later pass on to my family. It is no surprise to know what type of relationships I had, because of my beliefs. Those relationships became stressful because they were dependent on external factors that would create high levels of anxiety. Ultimately the thing I valued most, my loving relationships with my wife and family, would fall apart.

This judgment I held about how life should be was like the head of a river that branches into many smaller subsidiaries. Each subsidiary was a further distortion of thinking. These many facets of my main distortion consolidated even further my rigid beliefs. Unease was a constant, and I believed any deviation from my usual way of thinking was a threat to how life needed to be for me to thrive or survive.

Becoming aware of the limitations and imbalances that judgments impose on us is of paramount importance. Identifying the origin of a learned response to life, or self-image, can alter a rigid thought process to a significantly more open and reasonable one. *(For myself, getting a professional to assist me was one of the most important things I ever did. In truth, it was one of my first real acts of Self-love.)*

Judgments keep past lessons alive and well, separate us from others, and prevent our seeing how amazingly wonderful and abundant life is. Sometimes, a judgment may be delivered with an overtone of humor, and if it is said in jest to capture attention or as a bit of fun between you and others, so be it—but if the communication stops after the judgment is made, or if others feel hurt, this needs to be noted and questioned. Anything that disconnects you from others or from life needs to be questioned.

Even if a judgment is delivered in jest, or with a humorous tone … when your intention is anything other than for the recipient to benefit, this will subliminally create a disconnection—later (and it could even be measured in years), it will be sure to resurface, preventing an authentic connection ongoingly. Any limitation to authentic expression will leave others, and then ourselves, feeling alone. This is one of our greatest fears.

Is the desire for a loving reality a vitally important desire for each of us? I believe it is for the very reason that we want to feel more loved, more validated, and more accepted that we judge. It's as if we believe our judgments create that environment.

If we see in another person what we do not see in ourselves, as governed by our fixed beliefs, we endeavor, in an unnatural pattern of ego behavior, to bring the other person into line—so it can be said, therefore, that what we fear we judge. Or perhaps it could be said that what we feel is lacking in ourselves we attack. We judge others according to what we fear or feel we lack!

When we are judging, it is a sure sign that we don't feel good about ourselves and are desperately trying to overcome these feelings. The ego-self is our little world of a few square meters—how dare anything disparage its value! It is so easy to judge from this mindset—what else have we then but a few square meters in which to live, constantly comparing our lives to others, carrying envy of what others have or how they express themselves. It's easy in the absence of awareness to feel unfulfilled … it is, equally, easy to judge when separated from Self. When we are more focused on what we don't have than what we do have. To judge is to live blindly! Being blind to Self, what could we possibly manifest?

Why Do We Judge?

Judgments are a reflection of our past beliefs. We judge in order to do these things:

- Reinforce our beliefs that life must be a certain way … complying with a rigid viewpoint

- Control our limited reality … because we fear losing control

- Validate our expectations of others

- Protect our dominion ... the two or three square meters of "land" we occupy and the image we create

- Defend the images we've made of our ego-self—"I am better," "I am worse"

- Reinforce habits we have become reliant on

- Ease our own insecurities—we feel alone, unworthy, insecure

- Excuse and vindicate our feelings of separation from others

- Seek validation from others, win approval ... like minds strengthening each other's beliefs

ALL BECAUSE WE CARRY FEAR AND SENSE A REAL LACK IN OUR LIVES.

When we haven't adequately dealt with the origins of our misguided and limiting beliefs, we become fixated on the way we think life should be. We carry these beliefs for years, propping up and defending the image we made of the ego-self in consequence. Thoughts flow through our mind like a stream of unreasonable reasoning, with our behaviors corresponding with our beliefs.

Here is a simple example. We find ourselves driving behind another vehicle, which is holding up the traffic. Perhaps it is a large truck, or a car with small engine. We make the judgment that there is something wrong with the driver—they don't care about the environment or are inconsiderate to others. Our judgments easily trigger frustration or anger ... our reaction is a matter of course. The judgment gets even more personal: we judge the driver as infirm, too old, or oblivious ... "They shouldn't be driving at all! They are preventing me from getting to my destination three and a half minutes earlier!" What was the trigger here? Perhaps, if we look at it honestly, we realize that the judgment we made was a distraction from our own worries or concerns. It is effortless to blame others instead of facing our own misgivings and concerns, whereas it appears ultra-hard to face them.

This continual judging needs our observation. Through intent observation, we will ultimately see the extreme limitations that wrongful judgments impose on our life.

About ten years ago, I was particularly interested in the subject of judgments and their effects on me. I made a conscious effort to become aware of the nature of my judgments, their frequency, and their impact. The results were astounding.

What I came to realize was that my day was literally filled with judgments—thoughts about people, events ... all pre-assumed responses, and nothing factual, no intention to make things better or make the best of them. In truth, they were misguided perceptions that took away any joy or happiness possible in each moment. I quickly became aware that I had normalized judging as part and parcel of living my life.

I carried out an exercise of jotting down the number of times I made a judgment in a one-hour walk. In that limited period, I counted fifteen judgments. I'm sure there were others I didn't realize I'd made and therefore didn't count. The fifteen I did notice ranged from overthinking certain relationships, to criticizing colleagues for certain behaviors without any regard for their state of mind, to judging the weather, to judging a fellow sitting on a park bench holding a very large dog on his lap as "particularly odd."

On this walk, I also saw a relative I hadn't seen for twelve months—someone I had viewed as "unhelpful" after my marriage broke up. Even though he had been willing to talk, I judged him as "unworthy, unhelpful" ... frankly, I just didn't have any desire to talk with him nor any power to forgive.

When I realized how judgmental I'd been, I immediately asked myself the question, "How did I feel?"

How did I feel when my thoughts were consumed by my misgivings about others?

The answer was immediately obvious—I looked back and understood that I had felt more separated, with a heightened sense of anxiety, and completely powerless.

I observed that it left me feeling separate from so much of life, just creating more negativity—and for what purpose, I'd ask? Perhaps, in the hope that I might feel better?

How can expressing fear, feeling out of control, and continuing to judge improve one's day? They absolutely cannot.

Therefore, if finding abundance and more love and joy in your life is important to you, start to practice awareness ... And thereby learn, through simple exercises, to change fear-based behaviors into love-based ones, strengthening your new-found courage to manifest a reality that will unequivocally support you.

EXERCISE
Simple Observable Practice—Becoming Aware of Our Judgments

Take an hour of your day. In the space of this hour, begin to observe your thoughts and identify your judgments.

Often, our minds are not conscious of what we are doing when we are judging—it's habitual. Therefore, hindsight may be required to assess our judgments.

Jot them down!!

For five minutes at the end of the hour, look back to see if you missed a few.

You will be surprised by the outcome.

When we judge, we cut ourselves off from manifesting what we desire. Our judgments, we falsely believe, will help us achieve what we desire ... this is nothing more than an ego-myth of self-importance and false connections.

A judgment … is a perception—not fact … but fickle and erratic.

A partner of mine, someone I had worked with for many years, would readily judge clients or colleagues if they were not living up to his expectations. Yet he would completely change his opinion the instant he gained some level of acceptance or acknowledgment from them. He regularly fluctuated between, on the one hand, unfairly judging people and, on the other hand, condoning their behaviors if he was acknowledged or had something to gain from the relationship.

Have you noticed how quickly a negative judgment we make can turn around if the person we've judged does something that benefits us? For example, we might receive validation, support, or a material reward? So, the question is: what are we judging? Are we judging a moment of fact, or just a past belief? Are we simply judging others based on how we've come to view life—fixed, opinionated, and controlling? A judgment is nothing but a perception, created in the mind and readily changed if the judged person says or does something that benefits us.

The point is that we judge according to the perception we have at any given time: as rigid as our judgments are, they are also fickle, changeable according to what is or isn't to be gained. So why do we continue with our judgments if, overall, they leave us feeling alone or separate? Would it not be better to stop, reflect, change the thought, and feel new feelings?

Turning fear and unease into joy and peace of mind requires nothing more than a decision. Continue with fear and unease and feel pain, or make a decision to look at your judgments through new eyes—take the chance to learn from the distorted views you've held and gain the chance to practice seeing a different reality in an instant. Enjoy the rain; be kind to the man with a large dog on his lap—see him as the kind of caring soul the world needs more of; warmly greet someone you perceive as surly and watch the smile cross their face—then see how you feel; speak openly and calmly with your colleague about their challenging behaviors. This practice will inevitably change your life for the better, forever, by putting the power of life in your hands where it duly belongs. You won't always get the response you expect—but you will more often than not!

The separation created by judging others will always cause strain in a relationship, to a lesser or greater degree—either immediately or at some point down the line. Once you know what to look for, you can easily perceive this type of strain in relationships.

How many times have you placed people you just met on a pedestal, judging them as "worthy"—normally, in our society, those with money or success—only to feel disappointed later on when your illusion of them is shattered in some way? How quickly we can turn and condemn.

A judgment must be seen for what it is. It is a conclusion from which we create a position for one main reason: we are holding on to fear and believe life must conform to our set of rules in order to bring it into line or for us to fit in.

Why do relationships suffer under the weight of judgments, whether these judgments are viewed as positive or negative? Because they are derived from fear—they are built around a rigid past belief. With all detrimental judgments, their sole purpose is to gain something, not share something.

Judging to gain, seen as a positive viewpoint. When we say, "She's amazing and very successful," "He's my best friend," "I wish I was like you," or "I would like my partner to be more like you," then we appear to be judging people in a positive light. Nonetheless, these statements could still be viewed as expressions of a fear-based reality.

Let me explain. The ego can use a positive judgment manipulatively, making it seem as if we are expressing loving or authentic thoughts when really we are seeking, from an unstable egoic state, to gain something. If a thought derives from neediness or the will to gain something, regardless of how much we praise someone or place them on a pedestal, stress and pressure will develop within the relationship, and it will ultimately break down. Expectation takes its toll.

In hindsight, I have come to observe that "positive" judging behavior is an easy trap to fall into. If, for example, we are pressured at work and having difficulties at home, it can feel easier to relate to someone at work who is not connected to our day-to-day responsibilities—in particular when we have relationship troubles. This is probably someone experiencing the same type of pressures, but whose private life is outside our sphere of influence. Such relationships form because of common interests. It is therefore easy, when we are feeling in need of validation away from our daily pressures, to judge these relationships as "positive" or "authentic."

Yet often they are not a long-term solution—merely a means to validate our own feelings and behaviors at a time when we feel we need it.

I have also observed firsthand that it is easy to judge others positively if they confirm our beliefs, or we gain validation or status from them. For example, based on a perception of what constitutes success—say, in my case, generating more income—I made what I believed were positive judgments about others—those I saw as "good" money earners. I hoped my praise would validate them and empower them to achieve more, but it also validated me in return.

If we view success as having piles of money in the bank then it is easy to judge a high-income-producer positively, even if they are the most volatile or selfish individual we've ever met. Similarly, it is easy to judge a person's actions or reactions as appropriate if we have something to gain from doing so. This kind of judgment is how the ego manipulates its position: it uses positive judgments to gain something and negative judgments to avoid giving something away.

Expressing positive judgments based on the potential for gain or the neediness we feel can only fuel expectation and control within a relationship. Attempting to meet our needs through the judgments we make of others will diminish the authenticity and harmony of our relationships over time. The higher the pedestal we put someone on, the more we will expect from them!

Judging from a negative viewpoint. When we condemn, criticize, blame, hate—separating people by race, religion, education, or wealth level, we are looking at life through the narrow lens of past experiences. When we say, "We're different," "He has no idea how to dress," "They're poorly educated," "You're better than they are," "They are incapable," "She's weird," "He speaks too loudly/too softly" … and so on, we are judging in a negative light.

These judgments are hard and unforgiving and maintain our limited view of the world. They immediately separate us from others, increase the fear we feel, and leave us little room to reason—judgments maintain fixed beliefs and easily translate into erratic behavior. Importantly, they do not provide peace of mind!

If we feel judged, we often put on an invulnerable mask and heighten our sense of self-importance, separating ourselves from others, trying to justify and defend our behaviors, and holding negative thoughts that create unease. This consumes enormous amounts of valuable time and energy that could be better spent on authentically connecting to others and enhancing the quality of our lives.

Judgments are based on unforgiving thoughts, on an inability to accept life, or to accept people as part and parcel of life. In a real sense, we lack Self-love, because our judgments of others are only a means of outwardly projecting how we feel.

Judging is an attempt to keep or gain something. What it doesn't do is bring us anything of value that will enhance our lives or the lives of others.

Judging is a Revolving Door: Beware

The only way to stop condemning ourselves is to stop condemning others. If we become tolerant of ourselves, we also become more tolerant of others.

Judging is a revolving door that will always come back on itself.

I recall thinking, toward the end of my time in rehabilitation, how I would have judged some of those I met there had it not been for the confined environment where we all lived together.

On the outside, I would have been their judge and jury. I would look at others and judge them according to my very limiting beliefs about life and others, giving no mind to those I labeled as different from me, whether they were "drug addicts," "control freaks," "weak," "loud," or whatever else I perceived them to be—the judgment would have been made and the separation complete. Until rehab, I barely tolerated difference.

What were my feelings when I went into rehab and met so many people I knew I would have previously judged? I felt how separated I had been all my life! Workaholic, materially successful, now divorced, all along I had felt self-pity, frustration, anger, emotional ups and downs, resentment, hopelessness, unhappiness, guilt, and shame. Toward the end of my time I rehab, I experienced the opposite: peace of mind, hopefulness, happiness, excitement. I was excited that I had experienced what I did. I felt more alive, aware of new possibilities, and I definitely had more love for people.

"How could I have previously judged?" I found myself asking.

In hindsight, I can see that I was merely projecting outwardly how I felt within. I had never dealt with my past and didn't want to or think I needed to. I hid behind my success, endless activity, endless thinking, and rigid beliefs. In my adolescence, behind drugs, sex, alcohol, and any other emotional or physical suppressants lay the pain I felt. My feelings and behaviors were derived from my rigid beliefs about how life should be, or what I needed to do to hide how I was feeling. In truth, I was living a lie for most of my life!

On reflection, I realized that how I felt was no different from how others felt. My judgments had been holding up my distorted beliefs, and the more success I found, the more my judgments would testify to my beliefs. I believed in an illusion of success. Before realizing the truth of my reality, I would not have delved into my past to discover why, despite the success I had achieved, I felt so ordinary and lacked real love. No, I generally pretended everything was fine, that I was invulnerable, so as not to shatter the illusion that I escaped the past long ago.

Then I saw another reality. Prior to this awareness, did I judge myself, too? Clearly, yes; I started to really observe my thoughts and behaviors and discovered how often I had judged my own reality. For example, I would judge a failed relationship. The same applied to money: if I wasn't producing money, I would think, I'm not doing enough, I'm not good enough. This impacted my sense of self-worth. In short, there was no level of acceptance, only controls and expectations. I found myself expecting more rather than appreciating my life.

How often do we judge our lives? When life seems quieter than usual, or we feel a little more connected—perhaps because things have been going well—and then something small occurs that negatively impacts our reality, it is easy for the mind to work overtime to seek whatever it feels it lacks … to become a revolving door. Have you ever noticed this? That when things are going well in life, it remains difficult to enjoy and remain in the moment? We cling to the belief that life is a constant push-pull rather than a chance to appreciate, accept, and enjoy.

My separation from life and others kept me fixated on doing what I always had done. I was constantly thinking and doing and trying to get further and further ahead in business. I felt anxious, overwhelmed, and rarely appreciative of what I had in my life. If we do not face the past, the past must live within us and limit our reality. The present becomes a repetition of past thoughts and is obscured by them.

In truth, while I was happy on occasion, lasting joy was lost to the illusion that I felt I needed to maintain as a result of the distorted beliefs I held about others and myself. My judgments would trap my mind into a spiral of negativity so that I could lose any moment of authentic connection to life and others very easily.

Any judgment is a sure sign of an unloved Self, a Self that is lacking in self-worth, acceptance, and peace of mind. How are we going to respond to someone we judge, and how are they going to respond in reply? Judging is a trap wherein we fail to see our judgments as a sign of our own frailty.

Remarkably, when all of us in rehabilitation were stripped of our glorified self-images, self-righteousness, heroic status, and material possessions, left without our addictions to numb the pain, without any attachments or props to give us a measure of self-worth, what was left was our bare-naked truth. In the reality many of us had been living in, we felt that we needed external things, our props and distractions, to live our everyday lives. Rehab was like living naked amid a community of strangers. I found it uncomfortable at first, until I realized that unhelpful judgments don't exist there. Once I had this realization, my feelings of discomfort were replaced with hope, compassion, and a real sense of freedom. I desperately needed to find more helpful judgments about life.

It was soon apparent that no one is bad or "different," that there are no distinctions in addictions, and that addictions and unhealthy attachments form on the basis of an unloved Self. Avoiding the truth of a past that limits our seeing leaves us unable to manifest what we desire most in life, which is to be loved and accepted. Most importantly, during rehab I came to observe and understand that we are all the same and here on earth for the same, very important reason: to undo limiting past beliefs, support each other, and grow in consciousness.

Living with these people 24/7, I came to see them for who they were. They were drug addicts who had been off drugs for weeks, people with bipolar disorder who now had an ounce of support, people struggling with grief who now had hope. Others who just felt lonely and were carrying extreme anxiety had a chance to rest and find peace of mind. I came to see so many of my companions as beautiful, marvelous, inspiring, strong, willing souls from whom I took great courage—courage I applied to my own life. The love and compassion I felt for these people, after living without my former props and self-image, wasn't instant, yet their vulnerability and truth were endearing, their pain a mirror of my own.

My time in rehab helped me see a new reality of peace and love, authentically expressed and felt. In truth, how could I now judge? My life was no different from the life of anyone there—it was just that mine was more acceptable in society because I'd had financial success. I wasn't truly different in any way. We shared the same fears, concerns, worries, attachments, and addictive behaviors.

To me, my companions were, people I could learn from, love, and accept. I see them now as potential leaders of a new age. They faced their truth, and some were able to release their past. Regardless, all had had the seed of growth and spiritual awareness planted in them by their experiences. Their healing was made possible by the choices they had become aware of and could now make!

Relationships will be a struggle as long as we need to judge. How often do we unknowingly judge a loved one, based on our expectations and need for control? In any relationship, judging will function like a revolving door. It will swing back around to the one who initiates it. It must, or else how will we learn and evolve, which is our life purpose?

Love is not changeable. It is permanent and unconditional. It does not attack, blame, hold resentment, control, or manipulate. To judge, separate from love, is fickle, demanding, and full of expectation and the need to control, because we are judging in conflict with our greatest desire—to be loved and accepted. If we don't feel love within, we look for it in others—in all sorts of strange ways. When we connect in a loving way, we feel peace and joy, and experience more love in the most spontaneous ways. When we recognize this, we don't judge against love but for it.

Love finds compassion for others. Love heals and sees only the best in life, knowing it will serve us. It is not affected by prejudice, anger, hatred, or grief, yet it knows how to heal these afflictions well. What we have within us is what we will project outwardly, and what we will receive in return.

EXERCISE
Becoming Mindful!

Use the following three steps to reduce how much you judge and then ultimately stop judging altogether.

1. Do not judge for an hour. Then two hours, and so on. Increase the length of time after each success. If you mess up, acknowledge the mistake and try again, for an hour and so on. Then try it for a day.

2. If you hear someone else judging, do not validate it, and where necessary shed some positive light on the person

---

or subject. Feel the peace that can come from this—even momentary peace—and trust you will feel more peace in the future!

3. If you feel that you are the subject of someone else's judgment or reaction, simply do not accept it, walk away, practice silence, until you can discuss things adequately and calmly with that person later. Give your Self time to assess—non-reactively.

Letting Go—Simply Try to Surrender

Let go, stop judging, become an observer of your own reality. Letting go is essential to our peace of mind, our physical and mental wellness, and our connectedness with the inner Self and life.

To let go doesn't mean to stop caring;
It means I can't do it for someone else.
To let go is not to cut someone off;
It is the realization I cannot control another.
To let go is not to enable,
But to allow learning by natural consequences.
To let go is to admit powerlessness,
Which means the outcome is not in my hands.
To let go is not to try to change or blame another;
It's to know I can only change myself.
To let go is not to care for,
But to care about.
To let go is not to fix,
But to be supportive.
To let go is not to judge,
But to allow another to be a human being.
To let go is not to be in the middle of arranging outcomes,
But to allow others to effect their own outcomes.
To let go is not to be protective,
It is to permit another to face reality.
To let go is not to deny,
But to accept.
To let go is not to nag, scold, or argue,

But to search out my own shortcomings and correct them.
To let go is not to adjust everything to my desire,
But to take each day as it comes and cherish it.
To let go is not to criticize and regulate anyone,
But to try to become what I dream I can be.
To let go is not to regret the past,
But to grow and live for the future.
To let go is to fear less,
And to love more!
—*Author unknown*

When you are unsure or feel unease in your life, feel the love, joy, and peace that resonate within you when you choose an alternative path. Know that life is connected; each of us is a part of the whole. We can let go and accept life when we understand that our life purpose is to learn from fear in order to truly value love, for our greater good, in the greater plan of all life—for each other.

Healing an Unforgiving Mind

We cannot solve the past with the same thinking that led us to develop our adapted ego-selves; we cannot expect the adapted self, with its poor reasoning, to save or protect us. We must establish new ways of processing thoughts and feelings if we want to forgive our past and change our lives. Self-love and Self-trust are a means to put our fears to rest.

It is time to face the past. Stop our thoughtless reality. Stop just existing. Grasp life by facing our truth. When we truthfully observe our reality, we see which types of experiences and behaviors have provided us with sustainable, Self-fulfilled joy and peace, and which have not.

Each relationship we have is a chance for us to understand this more. To understand that only through authentic forgiveness, starting with self-forgiveness, and then trusting and surrendering to life are we able to stop the judgments and fear-based afflictions that limit our lives and keep us from the happiness and enjoyment we deserve. Let's enjoy the journey. This physical reality we experience is too short, so let's learn to really live and enjoy it.

Send subliminal messages of love, rather than messages projected in fear. Do not mind if no one hears the loving words you send. You are "reconditioning" the mind to new pathways of thinking, so the effects will be manifested later. You might think that makes no sense, but that is how change occurs. Life in all its forms exists only to serve each of us. Unity over separation is its only condition for complete enjoyment!

It is through our awareness of our experiences in physical form that we gain a higher level of consciousness. The more fear and pain we experience, the more we will judge and divide and feel further unease and pain. Through these experiences, we can choose to value and then know (through our desire for change) their opposite, which will ultimately lead us to the loving reality we deserve.

Isn't it good to know there are signs (and so many of them) that, if you are aware of them, can point you in the right direction? Judging is a sign. So, when you find yourself judging, be aware that if you want to see and feel miraculous change, you need to change the state of play.

Let's stop judging in the ways that divide us and send out the love that unites us.

CHAPTER NINE

PROJECTING—HEARING YOUR PAIN

"You can be right or you can be happy."
Gerald G. Jampolsky

Our mind's purpose is to create. What other purpose could the mind have, if not the task of creating? It has no arms or legs or bodily functions, yet without it a body does not function either. So, what holds the power?

We are literally creating in every second of our being, consistently; the laws of consciousness determine that there are no idle thoughts, each thought determining an outcome.

As physical beings, we have come to believe that we are limited to a mind contained within a body and that bodily desires and capacities are foremost and determine what we create.

Reason must tell us that the two preceding paragraphs point to a contradiction. We have come to believe that our inherent gift within consciousness, the divine ability to create, is limited and dependent on all external influences. But if the mind is limited and dependent, then is this truly a power, or a learned ability to miscreate?

Any power the mind possesses is gained through creative, free, abstract thinking. Power does not come from putting up walls, by containing the mind in fear-based thinking, or by giving the body power over it and making the body the purpose of the mind.

We underestimate our power to create, suppressing it because we are limited by our fears. When frustrations arise or we lack validation or meaning, a question that enters the mind from our physical state is, "How can we create a better reality?" Unwilling or reluctant to hear an answer, and with our bodily desires demanding immediate action, we look outward in frustration. We deny our mind's true power and thwart its true potential. We disguise the question with a whole series of other questions, never asking ourselves what the origin is of the fears that actually cause us to miscreate consistently, rather than finding the shortest route to peace and prosperity by looking fairly and forthrightly at the truth.

How many days do you wake up feeling a degree of fear? What questions go through your mind about what you must do? Do you have expectations of what will happen, or concerns about what you don't want to happen? Do you worry about facing up to what someone has said or done? Do you feel isolated and left out, and unsure why—or do you hold someone else accountable? Do you feel out of control? Can you recognize the fears you hold and the many questions you, like all of us, seem to need answered?

Of course, we don't ask the most important question: why? Instead, we project.

When we take a moment to reflect, we realize that our thinking doesn't really exist in the present moment. It looks either to the past—our memories—or to some future point in time. Yet the power to create only exists in the present! How can our thinking be abstract and free and unbounded, which are essential characteristics of creation, if we fixate as we do on memories and fears for the future?

Because fear is something we don't wish to hang on to, we project pain outwardly through our behaviors. What, then, are we creating other than a cycle of fear? As we project, we manifest more of what we project. The unconscious projection of fear and pain creates reactive or adverse behaviors in others, who carry their own fears and are equally unaware of their realities.

In the absence of a mind, the body is a functionless, inoperative, inert mass with no life. When the body is given power over our mind through memories (a priority shift), it is because our fears have us believe so strongly in the body's functioning as a means of survival. Believing we are self-dependent and self-reliant, we give up on the primacy of the mind and reverse its role. Here, our fears escalate more, because now we feel alone and unsupported and deprived of meaning in life.

Is it any wonder that, until we learn the alternative path, our whole fight is about validation and the search for meaning?

The body is highly demanding, unceasingly so. Its constant unmet needs determine what it is we create. These unmet bodily needs trigger our emotions and we manifest conditions such as fear, anxiety, anger, self-doubt, constant wanting, neediness—a need to control every aspect of our lives. Miscreating at every turn, we don't realize we have choices.

We respond thoughtlessly to the pain and unease we've normalized. If we do not change the manner in which we communicate in life, we will continue to limit our mind's true potentiality and continue to miscreate—to create a life we don't want, over the one that awaits if we look intently at the truth.

Effectively, we have lived a life with reversed roles, giving all our power to the body, not our creative mind. Through awareness, we are able to tune in to how we are feeling and transform our state from an unconscious to a conscious one, and thus replace our overreliance on external factors with an inner connection and peace of mind.

When we understand that our own behaviors are a reflection of our distorted thinking, and observe them and the negative impact they have on ourselves and others, we can begin to perceive these behaviors differently—and also, importantly, begin to hear other people expressing their pain through what they do and say. Inward turmoil challenges inward turmoil as distorted minds meet. We cannot release ourselves from the pain we have normalized, or its outward expression, unless we can hear or see the effects of this pain within ourselves and others.

When we consciously start to recognize how consistently we project our fears, and how communicating this fear-based reality simply brings us more of the same, we realize that our efforts until now have been in vain, and we start searching for new ways to communicate. As with all awareness, our insight gives us the choice to either stay with the pain we are feeling, projecting, and thus strengthening, or move away from it.

When we project fear toward another, we aren't taking responsibility for how we feel. We are attributing the way we feel to others. Blame, criticism, staunch resistance against having to look at another reality—it's easier than facing the truth ... isn't it? If we behave in this way, how can we expect to find or experience authentic, shared, and unconditional love or sustainable joy and happiness? And how can we find our life's meaning? How can we ever find peace of mind—life's greatest gift!

Projecting is a defense mechanism, in which we reject attributes in ourselves that we find unacceptable, such as our feelings of being misunderstood, unloved, or unimportant, feelings of lack in our lives, or the feeling that we are not good enough, and ascribe them to other things or people.

The ego-self is a mere distorted shadow of who we truly are. Each of us is a highly creative and free mind inherently connected to every other mind in the greater consciousness of all life. When we project fear, we are refusing to discover this truth.

We tend to do the same old things we've always done, over and over, as if each time doing so might produce better outcomes. We have built a habit of not looking anywhere for new answers or questioning how we feel.

It's as if we feel safe projecting our thoughts—fear-based thoughts that distort our thinking and lead to behaviors that have never provided the peace of mind or the outcomes we search for. Perhaps we feel justified, self-righteous, and validated, or our self-image is upheld, when we continue to act out. There are two simple questions we could each do with asking more often:

1. When have I ever projected anger and gained *sustainable* peace of mind or more love from it?

2. Has blaming others ever made me feel better for more than a moment in time?

If we are being truthful here, no matter how we feel in the instant of expressing anger or blame, even if the other person concedes, a residue of unwanted negative energy lingers and will return to us in kind either obviously or subliminally. A conscious decision to recognize the unwanted values we hold dear will significantly change the thinking on which we've always relied. This simple awareness, this *observation of our own reality*, can immeasurably change our lives and will genuinely provide us with the means to create the lives we most desire.

Thinking we can keep doing what we have always done and thrive, even though we've never gotten quite the results we expect, must surely be a distortion of truth. How will we ever actually feel safe or loved and nurtured if our thoughts and behaviors are creating situations in which we separate ourselves from others?

No matter what we make of our self-image, education, or status, or how much money we make, or what we have acquired, none of it will be as important as our desire to authentically and lovingly connect to others.

The complex manner in which we project our fear is an attempt on the part of the ego to look for solutions where there are none. Our ego-self is simply afraid to let go and trust that something greater than itself exists. To trust that there is something bigger, more supportive. So dependent do we become on the body that we refuse to surrender to the life force. This prevents us from seeing unity consciousness and the powerful effect we gain when connected to it. It stops us seeing a rich, full earth and forms a solid wall between us and reality: in reality, that wall is painted (perceptions) to look solid (belief) but made of flimsy materials (illusion) and in truth easy to break through.

If we do not feel happy on a sustainable basis, we must ask why. Why have so many of us been conditioned to believe that finding happiness on a sustainable basis is too hard? Is it because we are so good at normalizing pain that we simply accept it—or even see it as an odd form of happiness?

Like an under-nurtured child, in the absence of love and acceptance, or whenever we feel unsafe, we become self-protecting, deny the hurt we feel, and outwardly project the pain we know no other way to express.

Take the time to think back on your early life experiences—how many times were you disappointed? What experiences caused you to feel that life was hard and love conditional? What experiences limited your ability to accept life and enjoy the journey? Any traumatic events you experienced contributed to your set of values and your current limited beliefs. A belief is formed from layers of experiences that are repeated over and over. Loving experiences create strong, loving beliefs and responsible actions, while traumatic experiences create fearful, painful beliefs and then reactions. We try to get rid of these fear-based beliefs by blame, judgment, and denial and we certainly don't look for any evidence of the part we play ourselves ... Admission of guilt? No—we're too busy projecting blame or any guilt we carry. Survival of the fittest, or survival for survival's sake. Either way, limited trust exists.

Awareness is key.

Let's say that, growing up, we had traumatic experiences of feeling unloved. Now, in a present-day relationship, our partner triggers our feelings of being unloved—perhaps through a word or an action we perceive as unsupportive. What happens? Our past is thrown into our reality. We feel anger and aggression. Why would they do that to us? Our partner, meanwhile, may be experiencing the same fear and sense of being unloved from something we ourselves have said or done and be equally unable to express how they feel in a responsible way. Both are now reacting—no one is really listening.

When we learn to stop the reaction, to take a moment to hear what the other person is saying, and we aim to be considerate and kind over defending our viewpoint and needing to be right, we significantly change that relationship for the better. In that one moment we start to observe that anything is possible!

We must learn to understand the ego-self, how we react, and when, and how we project the pain of an unhealed past. Thereafter, we can own our reality and begin the real process of change.

Change begins when we take a closer look at our behavior and accept responsibility for our actions.

Imagine for a moment what you would do if you felt no fear. How clear would your thinking be, and how much peace of mind would you feel? Is having no fear possible? I have come to believe it is. While any of us can experience fear, however well-balanced we are, becoming aware of our fear allows us to make other choices— choices that restore the power of the mind. The body then becomes an instrument of learning—nothing more. An instrument of learning where the lessons of more love, peace, and joy are positively felt.

Remaining vigilant against fear and unease, we begin to identify our negative behaviors, a process that is instrumental in removing that fear and unease. I believe change begins when we are prepared to look at our reality and be truthful with ourselves about whether our projection of pain has brought us the happiness and fulfillment we aspire to. And if not, we must ask, "What are we going to do to change it?"

Internalized or Expressed Pain

A bit like a projector that's running an image on a movie screen, when *we* are projecting, we are playing out images in our heads that we believe are real. How could we help believing these images are real when we have become so engrossed in the movie we star in?

What we project onto the screen are our behaviors, which are byproducts of the personalities we have developed. The ego-self appears to us to be loving, kind, and compassionate, so we justify our behavior to ourselves, then wonder why others don't see us in the same way. Perhaps feeling misunderstood, frustrated by life, and overwhelmed, we attempt to keep up the act and fight harder, putting more into our "scripts"; or eventually we give up, believing it is too hard to improve our role.

We must find a way to accept life, accept others, and accept that all the good stuff in life emerges when we learn to accept ourselves as who we truly are. You see, there is no act or actor in the inner Self—it just is. When we connect within, we don't need scripts—our mind leads, our hearts are open, and we know how to guide ourselves through life and create the life we desire.

We each have a set of beliefs; some of these, or many, are based on our fears about life. And because our beliefs have no solid foundation, we thoughtlessly and tenaciously set out to find one! We all need strong foundations on which to build our lives.

In short, we become frustrated by and tired of the instability we wake up to each day, the ground constantly moving under our feet. We are tired of the self-doubts, the fears we hold about our relationships, the challenges we face at work, the highs and lows that we undergo, our concerns for our children's welfare and how they can get by in life, the ways people react to us, and our constant and exhausting attempts to justify it all.

We project our lives onto the big movie screen called life, where they merely coexist with other people's lives, rather than integrating … all of us just looking for space to be heard and understood.

We're looking for center stage, or for other people to give us a safe space in which to build our lives. But how could they? They aren't responsible for us—we are. The space we usually hold is so limited in size. When we are able to hold our own space within SELF—not in the limited view so many of us have—we can see the movie of life more clearly, and we recognize how utterly futile it is to compete for the little space we thought we occupied—the world then becomes our oyster. Barriers are dropped. Here is a strong foundation for our lives—unlimited and free, as the mind's power dictates. The space we need for life already exists within us; once we understand this, then external space is vast, shared, and unlimited in possibilities.

If we have unresolved emotional issues, we internalize our pain, believing that what is out of sight is out of mind. We may believe that others won't see the pain we're trying to hide. And often, we don't even realize we *are* suppressing our pain or playing a character. But our internalized pain will rise within us, like a wave approaching a shore. It grows in size until it crashes into our reality. Then it returns to the sea, adding to the volume of the next wave.

As relational beings, we depend on relationships for a healthy, well-balanced life. That is why our relationships are often our greatest catalysts for change.

In order to have healthy, well-balanced relationships with other people, we must first have healthy, well-balanced relationships with ourselves.

If we hold on to the suppressed emotional pain we carry, the wave effect will grow in intensity until our lives become unmanageable. If we continue to allow this to happen, over time we will get worn down: our relationships will be strained, our work will suffer, we will feel isolated, and old beliefs will be constantly tested and challenged, creating tension, stress, anxiety, and either a tightening of rigid beliefs or self-doubt and utter confusion.

Regardless of whether we believe we can hide or deny our pain, the wave effect can erode the fabric of a meaningful, loving reality. Our behaviors will then negatively reflect the pain we feel.

So why don't we change? We don't trust that we know how to, because we weren't shown. We're looking for answers outside ourselves, and so we play our roles overzealously in an endless search for ways to respond to the unease we feel.

Each of us is endeavoring to find out where we fit in life, and how we can find abundance, love, and joy. But we fail to realize that we have pasts that get in the way. If we do not face the past, then we must live with it and its limiting impact.

As difficult as it is to face, at some point we must come to understand that things outside us will never make us feel better for more than an instant in time. Even today, after all the work I've done on myself, on occasion I struggle to maintain this understanding, so I do my best to remind myself of this fact on a daily basis.

Remove the Past Through Forgiveness

Forgiveness is the path to peace and the bridge between the fear we feel and the love, peace, and joy we each deserve. It is the path to enjoying life to the fullest. Forgiveness must start with self, nurturing the ego-self, not condemning or criticizing it any longer. Self-love starts with understanding that our experiences brought us to this point in our life; we survived, and the ego-selves we manifested did a good job until now, putting in a monumental effort to protect the images we made of ourselves—for the most part, without malice and with good intent. But now, the same fearful self that carried forward the lessons of the past can no longer serve you or take you appropriately, lovingly, and abundantly beyond this point.

Accepting all we have done and experienced, all we have learned, has brought us to this point of heightened awareness.

With awareness, forgive all the wrong you felt was ever done to you, and look at life through forgiving eyes. This does not mean you have to dismiss what was done, only to find a way to forgive those wrongs. The peace you will find by doing this is beyond anything you have ever felt.

Through forgiveness, you will connect to life. Once you have forgiven, reactions are replaced with responsible actions. Anxiety will no longer keep you stuck in the prison of your mind. The peace and joy you feel will be a constant reminder of why we find the courage to forgive.

Looking back over the first fifty years of my life, I have come to realize that I had lived with fear, pain, or anxiety every day of my life from the youngest age. I noticed these feelings, but I mostly covered them up and defended my associated behaviors. As I grew older, those feelings intensified. I looked for more to compensate—more outer connection, in whatever way I deemed important to the ego-self. Yet no matter what I tried to do or who I tried to convince that my beliefs were the best ones, and no matter how much I fought for those beliefs, my attempts to find abundance were feeble at best, I now see. Even though I achieved specific outer goals that matched my definition of success, I never found what I was looking for. It was right beneath my feet, but I couldn't see it.

Why We Need to Own Our Reality

Our ego-self-driven behaviors are aimed at finding relief from our pain. If we do not take responsibility for them, we will not discover the "why" behind them. We must own our reality. When we do so, we discover the truth that exists behind the distorted thinking that in turn causes the behaviors that leave us wanting.

The more moments of peacefulness you can create in your life, the more liberated you will feel. You can create peacefulness by connecting in silence to your inner Self—giving yourself a moment to reflect, shutting out the noise and just listening to yourself from within. Because the mind is so consciously connected, if given options it will always gravitate to the path of least resistance. Options only come from awareness. We must keep practicing simple exercises for a few minutes whenever we feel unease, as we strip away old beliefs and replace them with new ones. Your mind has an amazing energy—an energy that heals! It enables you to instinctively know when something feels right or not, to find the path of least resistance and follow it.

If we are not taking responsibility for our distorted thinking and the unease we feel, we are not noticing the unhealthy impact our past has on us or others. We have limited our mind to the confines of a body. But if we stop for a moment to observe what is happening, it is easy to identify the pain being expressed. It's all a matter of practice in observation, feelings, and awareness.

When we do simple exercises every day to raise our awareness of our thoughts and behavior, such as taking a moment of me-time or practicing non-reactive communication, we learn to take real control of how we feel. This gives us the evidence we need to believe change is possible and accept that we can create change by feeling better through the choices we then make! Either we can be conscious, choosing to experience peace of mind, or we can continue to exhaust ourselves and only occasionally and randomly experience peace, love, and happy moments.

The power of the mind within us is so strong that even when we are exhausted from daily pressures, we will often be given a glimpse of a mind saying, "Use me for what I can do"—calling us to accept a moment of peace, instead of the madness. The constant stream of negative thoughts and reactive behaviors we engage in takes an emotional toll on our lives. Perhaps we feel sorry for what we have done or how we have reacted to others, including our loved ones, colleagues, or friends, or perhaps we have simply become tired from endlessly looking for answers as to how to live our lives. Perhaps a crisis has occurred, or we don't feel things are as we would like them to be. Or maybe we just throw our hands up in the air one day and say, "Enough!" In any case, at some point we look inside ourselves, to the inner Self, for relief. When we surrender to life we find peace, if only for a few moments. In these moments, we are restored. Sadly, however, even though we desire more peace, we do not initially recognize what has occurred. We don't seem to retain the little knowledge we have just experienced. In truth, we don't grasp how to generate peace until we become more Self-aware.

Inner Self-connection can be experienced at the oddest times. Think of a minor addiction you have. Perhaps you felt the need to shop after your insecurity was triggered, or after something or someone disappointed you? Then, when utterly confused and exhausted, did you take a moment to reflect inwardly, sit with your inner Self, and reflect on what had happened?

Confused and exhausted as you were, did you subsequently feel a moment of peacefulness and silent Self-awareness? If so, that moment was the moment of surrender and acceptance; your ego defenses were shattered, allowing you to connect inwardly.

Ego thinking requires an extreme effort from us, but our natural ability to return to the sanctuary of the inner Self when we are exhausted by our distorted thoughts and behaviors is how we "reboot" our internal computer—it is driven by an all-powerful, free, creative, and amazingly wonderful mind. Vacillating between ego control and surrender is how we live life; when we finally connect inwardly, it will inevitably be by choice, occurring when enough actually *is* enough and we start to ask relevant questions and listen to the answers.

Be conscious: use the following exercises to help you observe your reality and assess the truth of your feelings and behaviors. If we do not make a habit of observing our reality, then it is easy to lose a day, a week, or more feeling stuck in a rut. Practice these exercises often and your consciousness will undoubtedly expand.

EXERCISE
A Little Bit of You-Time

In order to observe your reality, give yourself a little you-time at intervals throughout the day.

This is a quick little exercise for establishing space in which to observe what is happening within you and around you. It's a chance to reflect for a moment on the feelings, behaviors, and thoughts you are having and assess why you feel the way you do—to ask, "Am I feeling peace or pain?"

When you are aware, you can create change! A moment of you-time will allow you to hold your reality long enough to turn any unease you may be feeling into peace of mind. For me, time spent in this way is essential for real productivity and sustained joy in anything I do.

Begin by spending a moment in silence. Sit down and rest. Close your eyes and bring your attention to your breath. For this moment, see if you can drop all thoughts. Try it right now. Put the book down and just rest your mind for a moment.

- For a moment, stop and listen to the silence.

- Feel your body, your breath, and your heartbeat as you slowly breathe in and out.

- Feel the life in your silence, and just rest in it.

- Let go of all thought for a moment or two if you can!

- Feel again.

When we hold on to the pain and unease created by our own negative thoughts, we stress the body and the mind and distort our reality. A moment of Self-connection can give us an opportunity to reassess our situation and accept what's happening around us.

Our projections impact us in these ways:

- Relieving us temporarily of our feelings of being out of control

- Bolstering our sense of self-righteousness

- Falsely empowering us

- Supporting our distorted reality, keeping us in denial

- Stopping us from looking more deeply at our feelings

- Passing our pain on to others

- Relieving us from the burden of responsibility

Our projections cause us to impact others in these ways:

- Blaming and hurting them

- Shaming them

- Judging them

- Withdrawing support from them

- Denying connection with them (although we often want the opposite)

- Disempowering them

- Manipulating or controlling them

EXERCISE
Three Steps to Create Love

Step 1: Love of Self. Self-love means that we value our peace of mind. When we are at peace, we are connecting to the inner Self. Here are some guidelines for love of Self:

- Maintain your peace of mind at all costs by valuing it more than anything else.

- Set an emotional boundary around those who disrupt your peace of mind, if necessary by walking away from them until the situation calms.

- Remain non-reactive.

- Stop questioning everything, and start observing more.

- Meditate or take moments of you-time several times a day when needed. Prescribe it to yourself whenever you feel uneasy, for just a few moments to start with and then longer if you can.

- Be grateful, truly grateful, for your life!

Step 2: Love of others. Showing love to others requires you to demonstrate responsible and courageous actions. Whenever you feel unease that's been brought about by what another person says or does (or *doesn't* say or do), either send subliminal loving thoughts to that person or directly express a loving response or action. Here are some helpful tips:

- When you hold another person responsible for the pain you are feeling, send loving thoughts. Remember, this step, like Step 1, is about your happiness. You are responsible for your own joy and peace. Let go of any resentment and anger you feel toward the other person for just long enough to view the situation differently.

- Stop worrying about everyone else. Trust others to know, or learn about, themselves. Let go of trying to control them and needing to be right. In these cases, practice the technique of being kind over being right. Be mindful not to enable, smother, or overly indulge them either, and give them room to think/feel for themselves.

- Do something loving; for example, spend a few minutes chatting with them or offering a kind word if they seem troubled. Don't enable them—try to listen without opinionating.

- Smile more often. Look people in the eye rather than looking away. Allow people to feel connected to you.

- Express love by not allowing others to express their pain through you. Stay calm, remove yourself from reactive, volatile situations, and return to speak about your feelings later. In the case of physical confrontations and abuse, seek professional help.

- Do not judge, condemn, or criticize others: practice stopping yourself in your tracks whenever you catch yourself doing so. Judging, condemning, or criticizing others isolates you from them and decreases your sense of self-worth and increases your unease as you disconnect. Feeling isolated may well lead you to engage more in unhealthy behaviors, or at best to regress to old patterns of behavior.

- Climb to the "summit" of your recovery alone before "throwing down a rope" to help others. Setting healthy boundaries to preserve your peace of mind and reinforce the Self-love you feel is important when learning new ways of perceiving reality. Often, creating distance between you and another person is an act of love for them!

Exercise continues on next page

Exercise continued

Step 3: Love of life. In order to maintain passion for our lives, we must avoid fixating on the conditions that do not satisfy us. Sometimes it is important to look at our reality and either accept it wholeheartedly or take a chance by acting to change it. Here are some guidelines:

- Stop complaining and start living.

- Drop the fear by accepting the situation you're in.

- Take a chance and do something you really want to do, something that aligns you with your inner desires. If you cannot change your situation because a financial commitment, for example, is preventing this from happening, then accept where you are for now. Through acceptance, things will change for the better. Accept the circumstances wholeheartedly! Attitude shifts always create change! Choose the direction.

- Observe life whenever you have the chance. Go for a walk and observe nature, feel the leaves between your fingers and become immersed in the smells, notice when people are kind and be kind in return, smile more even if you're not used to doing so; keep doing so and observe how you feel with this practice.

- Whenever you feel agitated, a little activity can go a long way toward enabling you to view your reality differently. Go for a walk, go to the gym, listen to a podcast that inspires, read a book. Don't sit, just do.

- Think about what you have always wanted to do that, to date, you have not done—things that don't cost much money are the best. Then do it!

- Meditate and connect to the energy all around you. Feel the field of energy shift as you allow your negative thoughts to be replaced with loving thoughts.

Replacing fear with love is essential for all of us. Love is our greatest desire, and its absence is one that no money, person, or thing can ever compensate for. Therefore, begin to question your fears and realize that these fears have stopped you from living your life to the fullest to date, and limited the love you gave and received in your life.

As we observe our behaviors and the pain we express through them, we prepare ourselves to change them. Behaviors based on fear prevent us from forming an authentic connection to Self, others, or life. As we replace fear-based perceptions with loved-based perceptions, our new behaviors will establish a reality of hope, acceptance, kindness, love, peace, and joy around us.

Allow yourself time to experience the immense benefits that come from projecting loving behaviors every time you are made aware of the pain you project instead.

Creating a more love-based reality can be challenging at first, as the ego tends to hang on to its old ways. The only reality the ego thinks is possible is one that looks outside the Self for answers. However, as the path of love widens and become clearer, it becomes easier to embrace change. Change that will bring an abundance of love, joy, and peace into our lives. This abundance we enjoy will be felt by others, and embraced by them; it is an abundance we may share with the world as our consciousness grows.

CHAPTER TEN

MEDITATE AND LIBERATE

*"It takes no effort to love. The state has its own innate
joy. Questions answer themselves if you are aware
enough. Life is safe; flowing with the current of being
is the simplest way to live. Resistance never really
succeeds. Controlling the flow of life is impossible."*
Deepak Chopra

We all possess the innate ability to transform our lives immeasurably.
Learning to connect to our inner Self creates the awareness that
remaining present in this moment is the gift that releases us from the
need to resist. In this gift, we feel happier and live freely. Accessing
present-moment consciousness and maintaining it will take practice,
but it becomes much easier once we make the conscious choice to
do it. It is our constant witnessing of the benefits that inner Self-
connection brings us that, over time, strengthens our belief and trust
in it.

Inner Self-connection begins with a willingness to change our
perceptions—to begin to perceive a new way to live. So many of us
are tired of feeling unsure and unsafe ... something has brought us
to question this reality, and in questioning, the inner Self begins to
take over the conscious part of us, and subliminally triggers our will
to act. It is when we drop the guard of our ego state that we become
willing to look for alternatives.

Awareness with willingness is vital for sustainable change.

The fact that you are reading this book shows you are willing to
contemplate change, change that serves you better, and aware that a
more fulfilled life must be possible—that surely we can do *something*
to access a more sustainable, more joyful, and easier path than the
one we have followed so far. This willingness or desire will lead you
to witness the many benefits in life or love that you may now choose
to experience; in this way, you will feel real control over your life,
thereby reinforcing your faith to continue—certainty arises because,

as stated earlier, your willingness or "will" to do anything creates new behaviors from new perceptions ... and thought that vibrates at this level (originating from inner Self) is the greatest creative power the mind possesses!

It is within the silence of Self that you can hear your inner voice speaking to you—the voice that knows how to respond, how to act, what to say. This is evidenced through the improvement in how you feel. You find yourself becoming more open-minded, taking a broader view, becoming more compassionate and empathetic, and a cycle of positivity ensues. But we must learn to *trust* in the inner Self and choose to stop believing in the many distorted images and reasonings of the ego-self. These are a taught response to life as we have come to view it, and in that sense they only *appear* to be real: they are not truly real because reality is only ever a gift from the inner Self. True reality is sustainable, offers joy and peace of mind, and is reliable—in this reality, our thoughts don't endlessly change course, because they are sure and certain. Sure and certain because their projections bring us the highest good.

EXERCISE
A Moment of Silence

This exercise is about acknowledging your feelings when you connect within. It can be practiced often; for now, try out this ten-minute exercise to help you become aware of any positive changes in your feelings.

Observe your surroundings—look intently at anything within sight, letting your eyes move from one item to the next. For a minute or two, see each item as inert, functionless without you, yet present nonetheless. This part of the exercise brings your awareness to the present moment. Let go of everything you see. What you see means nothing in the truest sense— these objects are only there if you choose to see them.

1. Close your eyes; hear the sounds around you. Let your mind become aware of each sound, quietly letting it go...

---

2. Now move your attention to the breath. As you breathe
   … follow the breath with your mind. As thoughts or
   sounds come to mind, accept them, then take the simple
   decision to release them and return to the breath.

3. Breathe deeply into the diaphragm, extending the
   stomach muscles to ensure the breath is drawn deep
   into the body. If you have a niggly thought that is hard
   to move, observe where it is impacting the body—a
   tightening of the stomach, brain pressure, or a headache?
   Breathe deeply into the pressure or pain, imagining the
   breath swirling around it. Exhale and release the pressure
   or pain with the breath.

4. Continue to breathe deeply and exhale slowly; six or
   seven times is all that is needed. Feel the immense
   relaxation from this one step alone.

5. Feel the euphoria, the deep relaxation … if you do
   this part of the meditation correctly, then you will—
   immediately! Quieten the breath … follow the breath
   with the mind, and the mind will become quieter. The
   path of least resistance—it wants to go there—trust!

6. Remain with eyes closed for the rest of the ten minutes
   (or more if you can)—release all thought. Feel the web
   of peace that surrounds you. Stay within this field of
   inner Self energy.

7. To finish, take several deep breaths and exhale slowly,
   eyes still closed.

8. Open your eyes and once again observe everything
   around you, for another minute or two—then go about
   your day.

The only thing that matters is what is within; how you feel
about what you see outwardly is a choice. Do this often and
you will start to develop strength of mind in detaching from
outer form, and become more reliant on inner form.

Meditation simply means a connection to mind. A mind that is free in the present moment, without any of the fears that can consume and limit it. Any activity that promotes an inner silence and distracts the mind from learned fears is a form of meditation. Meditation connects the inner you (mind) with the higher you (unity consciousness). The result is immediate relief within the mind (peacefulness, contentment, joyful feelings) and body (lower anxiety, blood pressure, and heart rate; increased immunity).

If traditional meditation is deemed too challenging at first, there are a range of other ways we can meditate. Active meditation involves repetition, and repetition grounded in Self can take the mind off worries and concerns and into the present moment, once again creating relief almost immediately. Types of active meditation include walking, swimming, gardening, hitting a ball against a wall … For me, walking each day is a very important part of my active meditation process. In fact, I like to mix meditational practices each day. If I wake up overly concerned and need an added boost, active meditation—say, walking on a cold day—with fresh air and prayer is an exceptionally powerful way of clearing my concerns and allowing my mind to operate from solid creative foundations.

I have learned that a combination of walking and prayer—repetitive prayer, saying the same prayer over and over as a mantra, and visualizing desired outcomes for the short and long term—gives me restorative periods of me-time, away from thoughts of the day-to-day challenges of work and family issues, and the normal physical issues we all face. Witnessing the benefits, as we surely will, provides us with the faith we need to regularly continue with the practice.

When the mind has a moment of reprieve from any of its daily pressures, the result can only be sounder or more reasonable thinking. When we cannot access that break, then a vortex of negative energy spirals into misguided thoughts and can easily culminate in a bad day, week, or final outcome. If we do not distance ourselves from negative thoughts, it becomes increasingly difficult to resolve the issue, and our negative thoughts often escalate into more.

Fear begets fear—love begets love. We need to stop for regular moments of Self-love to ensure that what we are manifesting into our reality comes from a loving and reasoned foundation, and not a fearful or distorted one. It is only when we can reason and think clearly that our outcomes significantly improve.

Following my active meditation, I find that a moment in silence to observe and be present with awareness softens any immediate difficult feelings. It momentarily rids the body of the long-held fears, and provides a certain inner trust. Meditation balances the mind and thereafter allows us the downtime we need to recognize what is important, and to create the willingness (willpower) to draw our energies into the service of our true desires. The practice of meditation allows our Self (inner mind) to adequately deal with any problem we face and manifest any desired outcome that has no roots in fear-based thinking.

When we invest our time in Self-connection, we are investing in our well-being to such an extent that our mind and health become stable through the interaction, and powerful through its reasoning. Stable reasoning will lead to incredible outcomes.

When we throw ourselves into the practice of meditation, the results are often determined by the consistency of our efforts. Our efforts are rewarded with feedback and this feedback shows us the skills we need to continue and be rewarded. When we throw our energy into surviving and living life through the distorted thinking born from past lessons, we ignore the feedback, our skills don't improve, and the outcomes worsen. When that happens, we lose motivation and see no meaning in the effort. It is how we have come to live life, and it is why we lose a sense of life's meaning.

Maintaining our desire for peace of mind allows us to connect, act responsibly, and manifest a life based on our true desires and aspirations, filled with hope, joy, and far more peace of mind. The mind is then operating from a stable base. This is what awaits us. It is the answer to our search for life's meaning.

Meditation will transform your life in immeasurable ways because it will give you the solutions to your problems, putting you firmly in control of your life and allowing you to manifest what your heart desires.

Active meditation can be a powerful form of meditation for an overly active mind, particularly in the mornings, when heightened, fearful thoughts are at a peak as we run through the many things that our day may hold. Not only do we benefit from the peacefulness of the activity itself—we benefit too as we shift our focus from worries or concerns that allow "no order to things" to a place of reason and logical order, and details fall into place ... often perfectly so. You will witness this benefit yourself: enjoying the morning air, getting your exercise (which also stimulates the mind), and creating order and reason will culminate in a peaceful start to your day.

Passive meditation involves working with silence and spending time in quiet and relaxation. It often utilizes breath techniques, mantras, visualization practices, awareness, and release. This type of meditation is the one most people are familiar with, and yet it is harder to apply at first. This is because we often don't want to become conscious of our thoughts—stillness is not something that defines an ego reality. Meditation or stillness induces thought—therein lies the challenge.

Passive meditation is particularly helpful in the workplace, or if we suffer with insomnia—working days and sleepless hours are hyper event-filled or thought-provoking and so the ability to maintain a calm outlook, remain productive, and create positive thoughts at these times will be highly beneficial. Active forms of meditation are less practicable options at these times—but rather than just allowing the stresses of work to continue, or lying in bed worrying, take a moment to escape the unease and apply a moment of silence.

At work, I would often escape to the warmth of the car, cocoon myself in the front seat and begin a twenty-minute meditation—in this way, stressful working situations could be resolved in an instant, and often were. I can assure you that taking this time for Self made me far more productive! So don't forget to tell the boss—many workplaces are becoming far more accepting of these highly productive techniques.

Sleep deprivation is another opportunity to meditate, and a ten- or twenty-minute meditation often leads to a couple of added hours of restful sleep—and bear in mind that a twenty-minute meditation can itself be as restorative as a two-hour sleep.

Over the years, since I began studying transcendental meditation in 1991, I have come to realize that for me there can be no law on the timing of meditation. I often break off for a period of five minutes of me-time if something particularly disturbs me, just to allow clear thought to return and access an alternative view of the situation. The cause may be what someone else said or did, and the few moments of inner time help me avoid reactionary behavior—now, as a result of this regular practice, reasoning has become the basis of my response more often than not. This helps prevent confrontations and their drawn-out after-effects of "he said—she said." While most practitioners recommend a minimum of twenty minutes, feel no pressure and start with brief moments of inner Self-connection; step by step, you can lengthen your sessions as and when you feel you need to.

I use passive meditation that includes the technique of deep breathing (as a mantra) to relax the mind and body and supply high levels of oxygen to the body. Once sufficiently relaxed, which deep breathing will most assuredly achieve, I direct the breath to wherever any unease is impacting my body. I imagine the oxygen circulating around the unease and simply release the unease as I exhale.

I continue breathing deeply while dropping or releasing all thought in favor of softly following the breath. Maintaining this process, I continue meditating until my mind adjusts, until it stops for even a moment any recurring negative thoughts, and until the breath becomes quieter or deeper, with the mind progressing to a deeper level of rest.

Following this process, I may use a visualization technique. Following deep rest, I bring into play my visualization of desired outcomes. Try it yourself—precisely identify what you desire and what you wish to resolve, who you wish to connect with—visualize it so clearly ... Circle it with white light, then, as your mind begins to awaken, release the desires along with the breath (as I released the unease, previously)—visualization and release. Release, too, all attachment to the outcome. To finish, use the same deep breathing technique as at the beginning, relax, and open your eyes.

Meditation is a highly powerful, transformational tool for inner Self-connection and a powerful manifestation technique. It puts the power and control in your life firmly where it belongs—with you. The more you practice, the more inner power you will possess. The more inner power you have, the less you remain in the grip of unreasonable reasoning.

Using a breath technique, releasing the day's thoughts, and visualizing inner Self-connection and silence in the evening will often ensure a good night's sleep.

During my time of obsession with all things external, on many occasions I couldn't sleep. Over time I found that, compared with lying restlessly in bed, sitting upright, breathing gently, and releasing negative thoughts (or dropping them) was far more relaxing and beneficial. By adding a visualization technique, I could easily discover options for handling any challenging situations and had faith there could be other outcomes. Meditation will cure the mind of its disorder because it gives the meditator confidence that they really are in control of outcomes. Time will prove this for anyone—practice and thereafter observation are the key.

If you suffer from insomnia, or maybe the baby in your home is restless at night, then be prepared, particularly in cold climates—don't resign yourself to lying there with eyes wide open, or lying in fear at being awake ... have warm clothes and socks next to your bed, ready to slip into, keep a comfy chair available, and make the effort ... you will find this practice exceptionally liberating, and your rest/sleep patterns will greatly improve and your levels of fatigue greatly diminish.

Here's a simple organizational task that will help you. Find that favorite chair and move it to your bedroom—or, if you sleep with a partner who might disturb you or who you might disturb, another part of the house. If you're in a cold climate, cover the chair with a warm blanket that is soft to touch and comforting. Make this your meditation blanket. Now when you cannot sleep you have a small place of comfort to retreat to, to find inner solace and rest.

Through conscious awareness, and my intent to heal the unloved part of me—the ego-self—and liberate it from the shackles of its many misguided and unhelpful beliefs, I became increasingly aware of the consuming thoughts and poor behaviors that impacted me every day. Yet, even though I felt hugely overwhelmed and fatigued, I still wasn't fully willing to change and witness the impact that any change might have—I believed that the world I created was so correct. In short, what model or mentor did I have? Not the action of fighting and resisting, which I had done most of my life ... but rather, finding a new path of surrender and inner Self-love ... a letting go!

When I encounter any behavior, feeling, or thought that seems to disturb my peace of mind, I now apply a steadfast vigilance to balance my mind and remove those fears. Not that it is hard to do—the fact is ... it isn't. During the day, I may just stop for a few moments, or five minutes, and sit quietly, breathing silently yet deeply into the diaphragm and exhaling until the body is relaxed, then directing my awareness to the gentle breath that takes away the thoughts that triggered the fear. What I look for within this small window is a state of no-mind—it is like rebooting a computer. Those few seconds of no-mind will in fact rebalance your life.

Often, I will bring into my consciousness my most desired outcome, but note—there are times when I want no outcome other than a moment of rest.

If your day is stressful, tiring, reactive, or uneasy, all you need to look for is a moment of rest and reprieve. Reboot that computer!

How good would you feel if you knew you had complete control over your reality?

EXERCISE
The Simplest Gift

Sit quietly for whatever length of time you wish—preferably at least ten to twenty minutes, or longer if you feel the need and are willing.

Try to do this exercise morning and night to form a habit with which to start and end your day well.

Also, if you work in a stressful environment, take any opportunities you have to cocoon yourself somewhere away from your workplace, for example in your car, and reboot your mind to maintain clear decision-making and capable responses throughout the day.

1. Find a comfy upright chair with back support, sit quietly, and observe your surroundings for one minute or so.
   Feel the comfort of the chair, and bring your awareness to the breath, breathing in deeply through your nose and out slowly through your mouth. Repeat the process half a dozen times. (Breathing out three times more slowly than you inhale will maximize oxygen flow into the bloodstream, thereby relieving the body of built-up stresses and anxiety.)

2. As the body relaxes it is normal for thoughts to seem more intense. Stay with it ... and let them come.

Exercise continues on next page

Exercise continued

3. Turn your attention to each thought, and then simply release each of them. If a thought persists, or other thoughts come, repeat the process—become aware, pay gentle attention, release. (We all need to go through this small battle of will. Stay with it. Be aware, draw your attention to the thought as effortlessly as possible, and release.)

We are looking for a moment of no-thought. It may last for only a small window of time ... but that is enough ... Feel the peace you will feel. If you fall asleep—good on you ... but always meditate upright, as we are preparing to consciously connect—living our life in the moment and integrating new lessons, available to us any time we call on them.

Next, savoring any feeling of peace, sit quietly for two or three minutes, and listen to the life around you—the sound of traffic, people, the wind and rain, the tree branch brushing against the gutter, the dog or birds outside. Just let your senses connect.

Continue the breathing technique ... gently inhaling and exhaling.

Take a moment or two in silence ... open your eyes ... remain seated, still ... and observe your surroundings.

Allow any thoughts to come to the surface—thoughts that cause you unease or pain, frustration or resentment.

When we are in a position to witness our thoughts, which we can do regularly through the practice of meditation, we have a choice to hold each thought or release it. When we release it, we are devoid, in that moment, of any emotional attachment to that thought.

We are creative beings with wonderful imaginations (amazingly creative minds!). When we relinquish our ego-self to the inner silence within, we are liberating this creative mind to create what is most beneficial in our lives, so our lives can flourish. When we liberate our ego-self through the process of meditation, thoughts no longer produce unwanted behaviors, which would otherwise inevitably escalate into drama.

When you first practice meditation, you may experience many occasions when the mind continually runs away with thought. Here's a small tip that may help at these times: it may be necessary for you to apply the power of prayer as a mantra—that is, repeating the same prayer over and over, to distract your thoughts. Then, as you become pleasantly aware of your Self in the present moment, with your overzealous thoughts subsiding or silenced, your link to the past fears that create these thoughts will also be silenced. It is a powerful alternative for an active mind that is being asked to sit with no thought. Remember, even a small break from the incessant thought will give your highly creative mind room to readjust and reason. A small window is all your mind needs to find the path of least resistance and the answer that works best for you!

Another simple and effective technique is choosing to simply drop the negative thought. As you are made aware of each challenging thought, know it isn't serving you at this moment, and instead choose to drop it. Like a hot potato. Then, bring your awareness to your breath. Allow all to be—accept all thoughts and feelings as they come into your awareness. Negative thoughts and feelings must be acknowledged to be released. They are better let out than left in!

Once you begin to practice different forms of meditation, you will find the method or combination of methods that serves you best. The feelings you experience will become your guide. If a given combination of meditations leaves you feeling better, you will learn to apply them more.

There are no set rules but the rule of practice. The more you practice, the more you will access very important restful moments. Meditation involves finding inner Self-love and acceptance, rather than chasing external thoughts founded on a fearful reality. Whatever meditation method you wish to adopt, whatever method works well for you, you need to expand it by regular practice. There is no right or wrong way of doing this. Do not put undue pressure on a strategy or a result … this is about acceptance and surrender. Meditation is about freedom—freedom is connection to Self and life in the manner we visualize, and then experience.

When we greet our negative thoughts, feelings, and experiences with kindness, love, and compassion, through inner Self-connection—and this is effectively what we are doing in the process of meditation—we transmute the pain we have felt from our many misconceived thoughts over our lifetime by undoing our layers of misguided beliefs one by one; in this way, we strengthen the inner muscle of our mind to disregard the thoughts that do not serve us well. This opens our desire and will to find a new path. And in that search, life will support our simplest efforts and provide us with a pathway to follow.

Life will support our every effort when we connect to it. That is why it is called life! Our lives are a part of, and one and the same with, all life … we are in our highest vibrational state when we make the effort to connect … Over time, with practice, the connection strengthens, and the effort lessens. Why? Because a mind healed of past lessons, by its very nature, finds it easier to find peace.

It is through our meditation that we will learn what is important to us—what we desire above all else—and find the peace of mind that will liberate our physical reality and manifest abundance.

The journey inward restores faith in Self. It increases our confidence to follow our heart, and to reject the thoughts that have suppressed our minds and limited our lives.

EXERCISE
Meditation and Visualization Practice

- Use the breath technique described earlier: breathe in, and exhale three times as slowly; this relaxes the body. If you find you are resisting, that's okay—keep going, or try again later … it's your call here.

- Imagine the pain and anxiety leaving your body each time you exhale (imagination is the key to creation … use it—it has been ignored for too long).

- Allow your thoughts to come to the surface of your consciousness (awareness).

- Step back into the recesses of your mind, and witness your thoughts … as you witness each thought, release it, or endeavor at least to have no emotional attachment to it (drop the negative thought).

- Continue to release the thoughts, allow them to gently float away, or drop them ... maybe try to surrender to your gentle breath once more. You will find yourself in a more present, more conscious state of awareness. At some point, you will recognize this by the peace you feel.

- Go "swimming in the sky"—choose your most desired outcome—visualize it (this gives me faith that I am being supported in the process of life). (See chapter 7 of my book *Silent*.)

- Visualize the outcome you most want from your day— see that day clearly in your mind!

- Shed rings of white light over it ... imagine it coming to fruition!

- Let it all go! Your thoughts are manifesting.

- Return to the breath.

- Sit silent in Self and be aware of your surroundings.

- Open your eyes when you are ready—go about your day.

Our liberation and freedom are found in observing the truth of our life to date, and we must have the courage to face it. Repeatedly accessing the conscious awareness found in meditation allows us to strengthen our knowledge and identify our misguided beliefs, by bringing to the surface the many fears that have limited and restricted our reality. Each time we see this reality, we are exposing a little more of the past to the light, until eventually we accept our past, and change our beliefs around it—namely, realizing that we are good enough, that it isn't right to carry the past any longer, that we are worthy, that we are not less than or bad, and that we are in truth responsible for our lives and have complete control over them.

Meditation is a very important element in our physical being. It's comparable to exercise or eating healthily. If the mind is the substation that generates all the power that enters the body, and the body doesn't function without it, is it not vitally important to feed it properly?

Life has been designed to teach us the importance of a healed self, and the importance of freeing ourselves to our greater consciousness—our inner all-knowing and all-loving Self. This SELF is conscious. IT IS CONSCIOUS AND AWARE of all life. It knows all there is to know.

A Self that remembers who it is and what it is here to do—that is, to experience every aspect of fear in order to truly know love—aligns with the divine energy of all that exists. The lessons of a healed ego-self can raise our consciousness and our ability to create more powerfully and creatively within our spiritual/physical realm.

Life purpose achieved!

CHAPTER ELEVEN

PERFECT BEING—
FLAWLESS CREATION

*"What can be more foolish than to think that all this rare
fabric of heaven and earth could come by chance, when
all the skill of art is not able to make an oyster!"*
Jeremy Taylor

The path to truth will give us each the courage to leave the past
behind, to undo years of mistaken perceptions, and to turn them
into the wisdom we gain from seeing them in a new light. We can
take what we know from our past experiences—observe them, ask
relevant questions about them—and, through our wish to understand
the link between past and present, unlock a door marked "choice." It
is all we need to discover … choice! It is with choice that the mind
will discover the truth … no other outcome is possible … to believe
otherwise is to misunderstand the amazing power of the mind and
believe life is limited. Far from it.

We will discover nothing unless we make the decision to step
forward. One small first step will trigger our creative and inquisitive
minds to ask more questions relevant to our search for Self-
fulfillment. One small step, and the mind itself will gravitate to
search out its highest expression … a peaceful mind.

A peaceful mind should not be an aspiration that is beyond us; it
should be an attainable goal for each of us. In truth, it should be our
only goal. Don't we realize yet where our lives are in this current
moment—do we deny that the world needs help and that each of
us is impacted by the way world events are playing out? Do we
deny the truth that our lives aren't as good as they seem, and the
possibility that there could be so much more waiting for us?

Why do we wait so long before we make the choice to look for
an alternative path? Is it because we are so fixated on the images we
have created from our distorted past lessons, and the beliefs around
those images, that we think … we couldn't possibly be wrong? Or

is it more a case of disillusionment with the world, leading us to say … "Our life isn't so bad after all"? Isn't this mere denial? We choose to accept less than our ultimate goal—a goal that eludes us because of our very unwillingness to search it out. Should we do nothing, because the world we see appears separate from us? We trick our minds into believing we are okay as long as we don't have to face any of these truths.

Let's take a peek at our past lessons, and at our behaviors and the feelings we carry, to learn how these past lessons impact our lives and as a consequence the lives of those around us, in particular our loved ones. Let's unravel the misguided beliefs one by one, until we free the mind, provide choices, hands held outward to grasp the change that will follow, and in that change choose to follow the path that will lead to our best outcomes.

It is through our poorly conceived teachings and our later awareness of them that we gain wisdom … and in that wisdom our spiritual evolution. Through our experiences, we evolve to a higher plane of consciousness, the plane of a mind that is liberated and peaceful, no matter what the world throws at us … A peaceful mind is our greatest quest, and through it we attract more love and more joy consistently … our life's purpose … to seek our heaven on earth.

Don't let your mind say it can't be done! To use these words is to remain limited and caught up in past beliefs, so that the world dictates the terms of your life and you have no choices. It is to say, "My few square meters is all that matters and I can't be affected by things outside it so I will hang on tightly to it."

We are fearful beings because we are relationship beings who are not manifesting the best of our relationships. It is our utmost and only goal to authentically connect in loving ways and feel that love in return. Every emotion we express can come from only one of two emotions, either fear or love, and every instance of fear is motivated by our need to be loved and to love.

It is worth pointing out here the difference between "needing validation" and "desiring acceptance." The need for validation is a constant unease expressed through an ego-self trying to find like-minded others to support its own rigid beliefs and opinions.

Acceptance, however, is the inner Self goal that each of us endeavors to attain—and the driving criterion behind all that we do.

The need for validation comes from the ego-self in the absence of inner Self-acceptance (fear based) and offers only short episodes of relief, while the desire for acceptance is a desire for a stable foundation in life that offers sustainable, loving relationships, peace, and joy through inner Self-acceptance (love-based).

We deny this truth, for fear of admitting that we need love. The ego was formed in the absence of it. Yet, we are relationship beings—and any separation from others will cause us discontent and fear. The truth of this statement is easily observed if we ask the right questions and carefully observe the answers. For example, when did you last feel most empowered, joyful, or content? Was it when you felt loved, or when you saw hope in the world, or kindness and compassion expressed by others? Did this felt response or witnessing provide a sense of relief from the hurt and drama we each live with daily? Love and acceptance are innate, born within us, within our DNA—ultimately, they are our complete existence, our mental drivers—it is the life that we are so divinely connected with that dictates this, and no other outcome is possible.

When you last thought yourself unworthy of others in some way, or you felt insecure, perhaps let down, did you feel there was no hope, that life was unkind, and that you had little or no control? Looking back on that time, did something extraordinary happen as a result of the negative impact on you? Did someone help you, or did you reach out to others and find that love and acceptance were there after all? In that adversity, did you drop your guard for a short time, drop the protective image you held on to so tightly just long enough for people to see the real you … and in those connections to other people, did you feel a real sense of joy, did you feel compassion, kindness, and more love? Did these feelings make you happy?

So, if we are relationship beings, with so many relationships and opportunities available to us, why do we feel so ordinary? Is it not because our relationships, including the ones we have with ourselves, seem not to meet our greatest desires—for love (authentic connections) and acceptance (starting from Self-love)? We are running on old fuel! Not green energy. The past needs attention—it is outdated and of no further use, other than the wisdom we gain in recognition of it.

We do not look at the past to relive it; we look at our past to forgive it and move on from it.

The adapted ego-self will fight hard to keep us from straying beyond its limited beliefs. We have made an image through a body and we refuse to challenge this belief—it is an entity, with its own body and brain (which we mistake for a mind) attached to it. A made-up self we created from our thoughts to protect and defend the world view we experienced growing up. The ego is thought, which comes from a perception of who we are based on past fears—from it, we have created an image and given it a life of its own. The ego's distorted thinking is therefore reliant on the image we've made. But remember, it is frail at its best, created from our perceptions and strengthened by our thoughts and beliefs. Perceptions that can readily change, and thoughts that can be undone. Where is the stability in this? It has no solid foundation. And if our lives haven't been fulfilled to date, and if we haven't found the peace of mind that is rightfully ours—then our understanding of who we are, behind the frail image we believe is all-important, is misconceived.

The ego is autonomous in its thinking (cut off from any higher Self or power) ... The self-image you made is the mind misconstruing concepts of love ... it separates because we made this image to protect us ... our survival mechanism ... us against the world—it is our lack of love that it has tried to defend us against. The ego feels insecure as it was formed without a stable foundation, just as a child growing up with trauma often lacks the skills to adequately handle life. It is our inner Self that knows love well.

Our inner Self was created perfectly for its greater role: to expand the consciousness and love that in turn expand the omnipotent divine energy of all that exists. Our knowledge of love is innate (we practice to connect) ... we are sure to manifest it in time and with practice, as it is the mind's natural function. Deep in the recesses of our mind, we each know that love is all there is!

We are not separated from this knowing other than by the ego-self we created in the absence of knowing it. We each need a foundation, a solid base on which to live our life—another gift of creation is to supply the means! Love won't fight or defend a position and merely waits patiently for our return. Fighting and defending positions is the ego's role ... it does so because it doesn't know what it is or what it actually needs. It is fickle, frail, and unsure ... we must recognize this in order to break the myth we created and move past it.

The secret to life fulfillment is Self-fulfillment. We learn through our misguided thoughts and actions, our fear-based thoughts and actions—anger, hate, unforgivingness, selfishness, neediness, separation, self-righteousness, lack of kindness or compassion, or denial ... and by realizing that these negative reactions have been detrimental to our lives, have offered us little more than fear and anxiety. When we realize this, we learn we have the choice to change our thoughts to ones that lead to responsible action, bringing us a sense of liberation, more love, more joy, and the ultimate goal of consistent and sustainable peace of mind.

It is through recognizing our negative thoughts and letting them go that our consciousness grows. As our consciousness grows, our love grows and our relationships greatly improve ... all our relationships. Yet it will take courage to let go of the thoughts we have clung to so desperately in order to feel safe, loved and accepted.

We know love because we are love. We are made of love, created in love and by love, and the communication between us can only be love, or else its perceived opposite (fear) will be experienced and manifested by our own hand.

Life's purpose in physical form is to remember this, to remember who we are, and through this knowing realize that the flawless creation that is life itself—one, whole, indivisible, omnipotent universal God energy—is held within us and evolves through the divine matrix (universal energy)—which is the ability to create more love. Therefore, it has no opposite. No opposite, other than the fear that is manifested in physical form ... Which, in the overall scheme of all-thought (unity consciousness), is in fact the tiniest of elements. In other words, fear is preserved only in our physical form and very little exists beyond it.

In fact, it is through the wisdom we gain from the fear we experience that we expand our loving consciousness. In this awareness, we evolve. We, as indivisible souls, are the highest form of universal consciousness—we are a flawless creation. In the wisdom gained from experiencing fear, what will we create? The answer can only be more love! As creative beings, our sole purpose is to create. In this knowing, the divine purpose of our physical life is recognized ... it is our desire and will to manifest more love. The sole/soul purpose of universal energy—and its divine intention—is to create love within an expanding universe.

Through knowing our perfection, we create more love. Now, if the soul knows love, being one and the same, then what could be the purpose of our experiencing fear as we do in our physical reality? Well, how would we really know how good our creation is, or how good perfection is, if we did not experience an opposite? We could still experience euphoria, have peace of mind, joy, and love as our companions, but how would we know them intimately? Isn't it fair to say that to know something is to know every aspect of it? Unless we experienced fear, how good would we know love to be within the perfection of our flawless creation? The divine matrix, the glue of the universe, the connecting medium of souls, is love. Pure, untarnished, vibrant energy of joy, peace, and bliss. Created to create more love!

Being perfect is who we are, yet we could not fully acknowledge this perfection without experiencing its opposite. In a sense, it would stagnate and limit our creative ability to some degree. That is why the tiniest element (fear) exists—like some divine plan of how to create more love and expand our ever-expanding universe.

Complacency is not a universal trait. Energy is. The perfection we can witness in our physical reality (earth)—the extremes of the earth's geography and landscapes, the heights of our mountains, the depth of our oceans, which support so much life, the extremes of our weather, the complexity of the human body, the molecular structure of DNA, the stars we see in the sky, all working in perfect synchronicity—is not complacency. Complacency is not life. Life, rather, is perpetual, immense energy operating effortlessly at such extremes.

Our inner Self is not complacent, yet we have come to believe so staunchly in complacency. Complacency doesn't create—it miscreates. We must learn to surrender to life and connect to the flow within life. Life surrenders; it does not resist, it merely flows. Nor *can* we resist; as the greatest and highest form of consciousness, we will be drawn to do our part ... we chose to do our part by living in physical form, becoming aware and making choices for change.

If the universe does not expand, it must contract ... it is the law of nature. If a tree doesn't grow, it dies. You have a life purpose and are part of this incredible journey for a divine reason. Your reason, your learning, your evolution are of benefit to the whole. We are each indivisibly linked. That is why we are relationship beings who suffer when we separate from relationships in whatever way.

We were created to create. The reason is that life evolves; like life itself, we must evolve, to ensure we forever expand our ever-expanding universe, and we do it through the powerful knowing we gain from experiencing an opposite to love. The divine purpose of our evolution keeps this inner desire alive. We live a perfectly imperfect physical journey to discover this.

Can you start to see the relationship of the triune being? The mind, the body, and the soul. The importance of this relationship? The mind knows fear to truly know love, and the soul creates more love through our physical experiences. Experiences shared and wisdom granted.

Now we have the masterplan of life ... in which we are all playing our part. A singular part celebrated as one in unity ... a knowing that your efforts ... extreme as they are in physical form ... play a divine role. The Self that is one with all others.

The world is growing old and tired from our poor beliefs; it is time to help each other regain our Self-knowing and live together peacefully and express more love. Fear is old; it is over and needs recognition and then release.

It is now we can play our part. What we give, we strengthen, and that is why we must evolve as single conscious beings to strengthen the matrix of all divine energy and thus expand it.

We were created perfect within a perfect plan to forever evolve and create. We create more of that which we are a part of, so that it is forever adding to the perfection that love is. Love is forever expanding, whereas fear is forever contracting. What we are doing could best be described as evolving our God energy. This energy of pure love is permanent, sustainable, peaceful, blissful, and joyful. It sustains life in all forms; it is the energy of creation itself, the energy of universal intelligence; it is all there is, and nothing else is.

The world is in crisis. Pain, fear, and anxiety are the consequences of this world's woes, and these common feelings generate poor behaviors. These poor behaviors are too easily observed and all too easily denied. It is too hard to face—but face it we must. When we do, we start the process of release. Releasing the past and embracing love instead.

We have all the answers we need to break the cycle of illusion our ego betrays us with. It is in the power of faith, in the miracle of belief in a life purpose, that we strengthen our resolve, prepare to drop our ego beliefs, and break free of our silly shackles as if snapping paper handcuffs. What awaits is purely governed by our imagination and desires.

We are so hardened to life, and as we start the process of a return to Self, the process of our healing, we face many barriers ... the fear of letting go and trusting being the main issue. The barriers that we encounter each day hinder us, and we react as a result ... but it is important to know this—regression with awareness is vital for our success.

Your intense effort, to this point in your life, has not been without reason, and the harder that journey, the greater the wisdom that awaits you. Accept it, and know that regression to your old ways (habits formed over years) is okay. Each time we regress with the added ingredient of awareness, we strengthen our resolve and our learning. We intensify our desire for more consistent change ... no longer will we be satisfied with fleeting highs, followed by lasting lows, or accept the physical world we see, in which so many are in despair. We will seek a more sustainable and consistent path to joy and peace of mind, not only for Self but for all.

We are not a body; we are each a mind within a greater mind (spirit)—a universal omnipotent oneness. We add to consciousness, as a divine right, so that we do not become complacent or permit consciousness to be less than perfect. Within consciousness we hold our perfect being within a flawless universe, being wholly satisfied. Love expands and it keeps expanding, because it fills the giver with love. What we give we receive, and when we give from the soul we are giving only love and receiving more of it. It is so fulfilling and satisfying that we desire more of it. Here is the perfection of creation. Giving love to receive more of it. It is the reason we all take part in the evolution of our souls. To be part of spirit, to add to it, as we were created to do. We are this pure energy in spirit and therefore cannot be separated from it eternally, just as fear cannot exist outside the physical realm, in eternity.

Our spiritual reality is real, not the illusionary image we have manifested and live with. A recognition of the limited fulfillment we have achieved from all the effort we have put into our lives thus far must tell us at some level ... there is more to life!

We live in a physical world and see with our own eyes the incredible depth and beauty that surrounds us, and still we limit our beliefs, our lives ... to a body, a short lifespan, and then death ... where is the purpose or meaning to this? Where is the connection between our self and the beauty and magnitude that exist around us?

Keep the faith that there is more than what we have made of our world in crisis.

We are one with everything else; we will remember this on the day we pass from our body and return to our true reality. This is the place, the only place, that holds our full understanding of all the answers that we have ever asked for, and, gained through our experience, our knowledge of all that we are, where we are from, and what we are a part of. The place of pure love, peace, and joy, forever permanent in our reality. Our true and only reality.

In essence, we have no choice but to return to the loving energy we call our higher power. We are an essential, indivisible part of this higher power. And it is part of us, just as oxygen is part of this physical world. We must return to it for we have never left it. To leave it would be impossible because we are not the creator of it, we were created by it.

Our role is to evolve with it by adding light and love; this is our role within creation. Part of the universal plan. We are the plan, we live the plan, we evolve with the plan, we aspire to the plan; the plan is for every one of us to find our way back to the knowledge of who we are, so that we forever expand the light and love that is the creative power of everything in existence. It is itself the sustenance and continuation of the plan.

So, when we arrive at this point of choice, and look for a path away from the fear and pain we have made of our lives, we must then withstand the physical pain of undoing years of traumatic experiences, of the layers upon layers of conditioned hurts and worries. As we approach our healing, and thereafter our remembering, the truth of our past leads us to identify our pain, and as we access and then release each aspect of pain, we revisit and relive it. This is the challenge of the early stages of healing: we simply do not wish to revisit it. Yet our physical form is the only place where we *can* start to face up to our past, and in that facing up identify the truth of that past, and the pain and fear we have lived by and have been teaching to those we love. Our world will implode, no matter how we believe we can protect it, if we are not honest about all the ways we have separated ourselves from Self and others.

It is a time when we need to call on our inner Self for guidance and truth. It will take courage to face the truth, as the truth is painful for anyone to bear. The undoing of untruth will hurt, and each time we experience it we will want to run and hide, just like we have done all our life. But the mere scraps of joy we have received so far in life have been unfulfilling. We need answers. Now we are asking for more—we are asking for what we deserve!

This "more" is found in the truths we discover when we observe our reality, and it is accessed through feeling. Through our feelings, we will come to know what it is we are thinking, and whether that thinking is good or bad for us. Any pain we feel will be part of our answer.

Do not turn back when the process starts. When we gather the intent for change, we must remain aware and vigilant against old patterns of behavior that will whisk us back to familiar territory— the place where we feel safe; yet we know deep within that our ego-self can never offer us the treasure we seek. Our peace of mind can only be found in the inner silence of Self. And it is to here that we must return. In order to maintain Self-awareness, we must be ever alert to our feelings, as our feelings are our conduit to our thoughts.

We are responsible for how we react to the world, and it is how we act toward the world and those within it that can shift us from the perception of despair to the reality of hope. Our reality determines how we see the world. The inner Self has no other way of seeing the world than through love and hope; it is within the inner Self that the ego-self and the illusion we play out lose their grip on us. They are lost to the light of this consciousness—an inherent knowing that we are much bigger than the few square meters we live within.

Created perfect, we were born into imperfection to know such perfection! Our life purpose!

How wonderful our gifts, how important we are, in the greater plan of all life. The perfection and expansion of consciousness. As part of that expansion, we experience a life in time—a finite period, the opposite of what we really are—to fully appreciate and understand who we are and why we are here.

We are given the gift of being created to manifest whatever we choose. We each chose our life, and in so doing found the path to more love. Every person we meet or come into contact with is another opportunity to express this. Acceptance of our life purpose is only a matter of time.

The chance meetings, the intimate relationships, in each instant give us the opportunity to remember who we are. When we choose unity over separation, when we choose to play our part ... we are choosing love over fear. It is here that love can be freely and fearlessly expressed.

The truth is that love is all there is—embrace it. We cannot fear it any longer, nor can we make the excuse that there is no purpose or meaning to this life. That is how life has gotten us to this point ... to believing there is no purpose. Who wants to live without purpose? No one, I'm sure.

Until now, perhaps nothing you have thought has offered you any sustainable love and joy in your life—but when you choose a different path, the light of your consciousness reveals your unconscious past, releases you from its disillusionment, and helps you see a perfect being within a flawless creation.

To know your Self is to look back on your life and realize there was purpose to it all, and that purpose is the gift we now share with each other and those we say we love.

About the Author

Gregory Nicholas Malouf became one of Australia's leading business entrepreneurs, employing hundreds of people, and was at the top of the real estate and development industry. Gregory's first book, *Silent*, captured his realization that this external success was merely a reaction to internal struggles, built on a desire to escape his traumatic past ... a past Greg would never escape until he realised there was a better way!

Greg now divides his time between Australia and the UK. Work brought him to the UK, where he co-founded the development group appointed to the £5 billion inner-city/waterfront regeneration programme in Liverpool, England.

Milton Keynes UK
Ingram Content Group UK Ltd.
UKHW021031160324
439500UK00005B/33